LAS VEGAS
WITH KIDS

LAS VEGAS WITH KIDS

Where to Go, What to Do in America's Hottest Family Destination

Barbara Land

PRIMA PUBLISHING

PRIMA PUBLISHING and its colophon, which consists of the letter P over PRIMA, are registered trademarks of Prima Communications, Inc.

Library of Congress Cataloging-in-Publication Data

Land, Barbara.
    Las Vegas with kids : where to go, what to do in America's hottest family destination / Barbara Land.
        p   cm.
    Includes index.
    ISBN 0-7615-0014-6 (paperback)
    1. Las Vegas (Nev.)—Guidebooks.   2. Family recreation—Nevada—Las Vegas—Guidebooks.   3. Children—Travel—Nevada—Las Vegas—Guidebooks.   I. Title.
F849.L35L34   1995
917.93'1350433—dc20   95-2703
                                                        CIP

95 96 97 98 99 AA 10 9 8 7 6 5 4 3 2 1
Printed in the United States of America

How to Order:
Single copies may be ordered from Prima Publishing, P.O. Box 1260BK, Rocklin, CA 95677; telephone (916) 632-4400. Quantity discounts are also available. On your letterhead, include information concerning the intended use of the books and the number of books you wish to purchase.

Contents

Contents

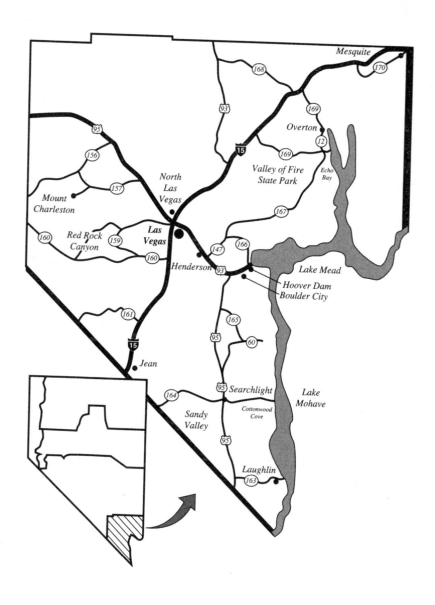

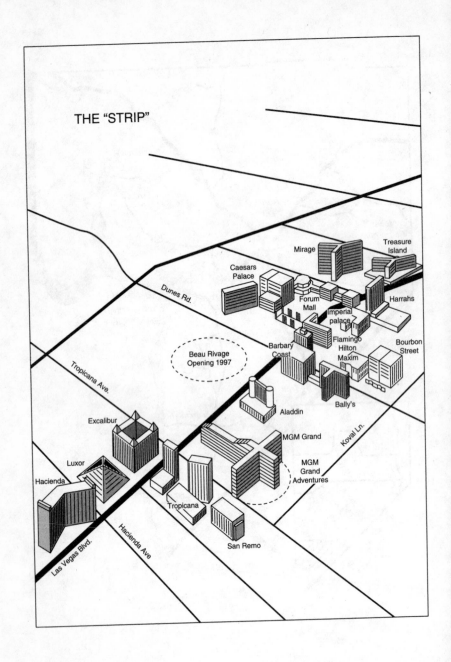

THE "STRIP"

Mirage

Treasure Island

Caesars Palace

Forum Mall

Imperial palace

Harrahs

Dunes Rd.

Flamingo Hilton

Bourbon Street

Beau Rivage Opening 1997

Barbary Coast

Maxim

Tropicana Ave.

Aladdin

Bally's

Excalibur

MGM Grand

Koval Ln.

Luxor

MGM Grand Adventures

Hacienda

Tropicana

Las Vegas Blvd.

Hacienda Ave

San Remo

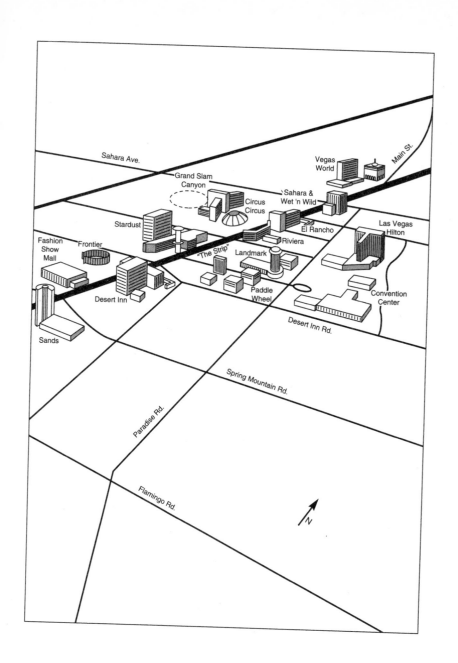

1

Fun in the City

CHAPTER 1

A Family Vacation Includes the Kids

It's all true. Everything you've heard and read about Las Vegas is true for millions of vacationers who swarm through the city every year. Whatever they expect to find, they usually find it . . . and a lot of surprises, too.

They come here to explore glittering resorts on the Las Vegas Strip, to test their luck in casinos, and to lounge in the sunshine beside shimmering pools. They applaud extravagant stage productions in the showrooms; they sample inexhaustible menus from lavish buffets. And now that more and more parents are bringing their children to Las Vegas, kids are telling friends at home about a growing list of attractions designed especially for young visitors.

Toddlers and teens join the crowds at theme resorts to sample virtual reality adventures and laser-light illusions. On moving sidewalks and a brand new monorail, families are whisked from one fantastic attraction to the next. While walking down the Strip, they may witness a pirate battle, watch a volcano erupt, or see a fire-breathing dragon slain by King Arthur's magician. Inside the resorts, they find talking statues, tropical birds, and live tigers. In a special habitat, they meet dolphins face-to-face.

Beyond the Strip, these families find room to move in green parks and museums designed with kids in mind. Some venture outside the city to hike or camp in the rocky desert, to ski in the mountains, to sail on Lake Mead. Some are there to study desert rocks and wildlife. Others dig into the past, uncovering secrets of the Ancient Ones who lived in the desert long before the neon city existed.

Possibilities and variations seem endless for these travelers. Now that you're planning your own Las Vegas vacation, maybe you can pick up a few tips from somebody else's experience.

A THREE-DAY ADVENTURE ... WITH KIDS

A few months ago, accompanied by two children who'd never been to Las Vegas, I revisited my favorite spots, discovered some new ones, and found out what kids liked best. We knew we couldn't see it all in just three days, so I let them choose the places they'd heard about and didn't want to miss.

At the MGM Grand, we explored a mini-Disneyland in the thirty-three-acre theme park behind the casino. We tested the Lightning Bolt and Grand Canyon Rapids, and joined a Deep Earth Exploration team in a simulated-motion theater. We ate crab cakes and hamburgers on the *Cotton Blossom* riverboat and wandered through streets that led us from Old New York to Casablanca Plaza to the Salem Waterfront, then to Paris, Hollywood, and the Wild West via an Asian village. On a side trip to the Emerald City, we renewed our acquaintance with Dorothy, Toto, the Cowardly

Lion, the Scarecrow, and the Tin Man—all our old friends from the Land of Oz.

At Excalibur we were spectators at King Arthur's Tournament, where armored knights on horseback jousted with lances, and Merlin the Magician was ringmaster for performances by acrobats, dancers, and trick riders. Outdoors beside the castle moat, we watched Merlin subdue a fifty-one-foot fire-breathing robotic dragon.

Inside the Luxor, a thirty-story glass-covered pyramid guarded by a giant sphinx, we crossed the "River Nile," where visitors traveled by barge around the pyramid's perimeter. As we roamed through an entertainment atrium big enough to hold nine Boeing 747s, we wished we had all day to sample the simulated-motion rides and high-tech games. Forcing ourselves to make choices, we bought tickets to the middle episode of "Secrets of the Luxor Pyramid," and later explored a replica of King Tut's tomb.

Another day, at the Mirage, we visited live dolphins in their protected habitat and watched white tigers prowl through rocky caves, their temporary quarters between performances with magicians Siegfried and Roy. After dark, surrounded by crowds of curious sight-seers on the sidewalk outside the Mirage, we held our breath as a tropical volcano erupted in a blazing shower of fireworks.

Next door, outside Treasure Island, a sea battle exploded on Buccaneer Bay. A British frigate fired its cannons at a pirate ship, and the brigands fired back. Seamen and pirates treated the sidewalk audience to an acrobatic display, swinging from ropes, shinnying up tall masts, and leaping into the water. Inside, we found pirate treasures in the shops, games at Mutiny Bay, good food in the restaurants, and bright, spacious hotel rooms for our three nights in Las Vegas.

At Caesars Forum, talking statues of Roman gods seemed to come to life under a stormy sky. The lavish shops were tempting, but the clock was ticking—no time to explore Planet Hollywood or see a show in the dome-shaped Omnimax Theater. We had only three days to see *everything* and we hadn't ventured more than halfway up Las Vegas Boulevard.

We hadn't yet visited Grand Slam Canyon at Circus Circus or Wet 'n' Wild water park or the Magic & Movie Hall of Fame. We hadn't looked beyond the entertainment resorts to the Lied Discovery Children's Museum, the Natural History Museum, and the Old Mormon Fort. Dozens of attractions competed for our limited time, and we wanted to reserve some of that time for outdoor exploring.

OUTSIDE THE CITY

Should we drive fifty miles northeast to the Valley of Fire? If we did, we could stop at Overton to see remains of an ancient Indian civilization in the Lost City Museum. Should we book a one-day sight-seeing flight to the Grand Canyon? Or should we head west to the geological wonders of Red Rock Canyon National Conservation Area, just seventeen miles from downtown Las Vegas?

It was August. The temperature outside our hotel was 110° F. Much too hot for rock climbing. We'd heard that people actually *ski* on nearby Mt. Charleston . . . but not in the summer. We'd simply have to postpone some Las Vegas adventures until another time. So we agreed to spend part of one day away from the city at Lake Mead and Hoover Dam.

The dam, a mammoth man-made wonder of engineering, is twenty miles east of Las Vegas at Black Rock Canyon on the border between Nevada and Arizona. We wanted to see Lake Mead, one of the world's largest artificial lakes, created sixty years ago when Hoover Dam first began harnessing the power of the Colorado River.

As soon as we entered the Lake Mead National Recreation Area, we knew we couldn't begin to see it all—not in a day or a week or a lifetime. Lake Mead itself is 115 miles long, with 550 miles of shoreline meandering through two states. The surrounding park, about twice the size of Rhode Island, extends from the north edge of Grand Canyon National Park in Arizona to a point 67 miles south of Hoover Dam.

At the Alan Bible Visitor Center, about four miles east of Boulder City, we found friendly park rangers and brochures describing recreational possibilities in the area. Some nine million visitors, we learned, come to Lake Mead every year. Hikers and campers flock to six developed sites on the lake. So do fishermen and boaters, water-skiers, and sailboarders. "Junior Ranger" programs are offered for children during the school year, and the *Desert Lake View* newspaper offers bits of nature lore, history, safety tips, and lists of facilities and services.

In the August heat, we settled for natural history exhibits inside the air-conditioned Visitor Center and a stroll around the small cactus garden outside. A few minutes later, feeling tiny as insects, we were standing in the sun at the top of massive Hoover Dam, looking down more than seven hundred feet to the river below. Busloads of visitors arrived, crowding into elevators that carried them down into the power plant for a guided tour. Others rushed to the exhibit building at the west end of the dam to see a model of the river basin.

On our way back to Treasure Island, we talked about all the things we wanted to do the "next time we're in Las Vegas" and promised ourselves another visit. After the children went home with their parents, I stayed two more days, long enough to explore the new Lied Discovery Children's Museum, the Natural History

Museum, and a few more attractions on the Las Vegas Strip.

Weeks later, about halfway through the writing of this book, I returned to Las Vegas for more exploration, this time interviewing children everywhere I went. The lasting impression I brought home with me is a chorus of young voices calling the place "Neat!" . . . "Great!" . . . "Awesome!" The consensus seems to be: "We want to come back."

WHAT YOU'LL FIND IN THIS BOOK

To help you plan your own family adventure in Las Vegas, this book provides a menu of entertainment, museums, restaurants, hotels, and daytrips. Beginning with the new and famous mega-resorts on Las Vegas Boulevard we follow a logical route from south to north, visiting Luxor and Excalibur, the MGM Grand, Caesars Palace, the Mirage, Treasure Island, and Grand Slam Canyon at Circus Circus.

Other attractions on the Strip—including Wet 'n' Wild, Virtual World, and the Imperial Palace Auto Collection—will fall into place along the way. You know you can't see everything at once, but you can choose highlights that appeal most to your family. Once you're there, you'll follow your own best path, depending upon the location of your hotel. Maps will help you find what you're looking for.

Off the Strip, we look into museums and parks and the University of Nevada Las Vegas campus. We visit some historic landmarks "downtown" and the oasis where it all began. You'll learn about special tours for children and possible daytrips to the Grand Canyon,

Lake Mead, Valley of Fire, Red Rock Canyon, and neighboring desert ghost towns.

Scattered through these chapters, you'll find lists of hotels, restaurants, shops, and churches with addresses and telephone numbers. Chapter 7 gives a rundown on the shopping scene; chapter 8 tells you where to find specific international influences and about the many ethnic origins of Las Vegans.

Section 3, comprising the last three chapters, begins with suggestions for planning ahead—arrangements you can and should make before you leave home. Chapter 15 includes travel information (Will you fly or drive? Arrive by bus or train?) and tips for getting around the city, with or without a car. Special arrangements are easy if you know where to call. Chapter 16 gives you on-the-spot advice in a hurry: information about wheelchair access, medical attention, babysitters, and hotels where you can bring the family pet, as well as some emergency numbers.

By the time you've finished reading, you'll have a good idea about some of the things you and your family want to do in Las Vegas. Some arrangements should be made in advance, but your entertainment itinerary will plan itself. Be prepared for some surprises!

Chapter 2

Luxor and Excalibur Theme Resorts

Even before you land at McCarran International Airport, you can see one thing that makes this city different. Space! Lots of it. Space surrounds the city and spreads between fantastic buildings. You've flown across miles of crumpled desert. Now you see green lawns and trees below and sparkling towers in the distance. Unlike the skyscrapers in older and bigger cities, these are not crowded together. Some sprawling structures occupy separate, distinctive oases.

As the plane descends, the pilot identifies a few landmarks on Las Vegas Boulevard, the street known around the world as "the Strip." There's Caesars Palace—the one with formal gardens and fountains—and the shimmering Mirage, with Treasure Island next door. (Can you spot the pirate ships on Buccaneer Bay?) Farther north a giant pink dome covers Grand Slam Canyon at Circus Circus.

To the south, there's the emerald green expanse of the MGM Grand and its adjoining theme park.

Across Las Vegas Boulevard from the MGM Grand and the neighboring Tropicana, the white medieval turrets of Excalibur reach toward the sky. And you can't miss that bronze-colored glass pyramid near the south end of the Strip. Luxor, the pyramid-shaped resort named for an Egyptian city, seems somehow right at home in the Nevada desert.

One of these fantasy resorts may be your destination. After landing, you'll discover at ground level how close the airport is to the Strip. You can see Luxor and Excalibur from the airport terminal. Whether you get there by taxi, airport van, bus, or rented car, you can reach the southernmost hotels in less than ten minutes.

Luxor and Excalibur . . . ancient Egypt and Camelot . . . each promises its own illusions. Both resorts belong to Circus Circus Enterprises, a giant entertainment-and-gaming company built around the original Circus Circus, opened on the Strip in 1968. The two newer theme resorts came along more recently: Excalibur in 1990 and Luxor in 1993. Hotel accommodations in the pyramid are more expensive than those at the castle, but children twelve and under stay free at either resort. Both offer entertainment for families, and you don't have to be a hotel guest to enjoy the games, shows, restaurants, and shops.

ANCIENT EGYPT—THEN AND NOW

On our systematic, south-to-north tour of the Strip, Luxor Las Vegas is the logical starting point. The pyramid is waiting majestically at the end of an avenue of royal palms.

Luxor Hotel/Casino
3900 Las Vegas Boulevard
Las Vegas, NV 89119-1000
Room reservations: (800) 288-1000
Inside Nevada: (702) 262-4000
Fax: (702) 626-4404
Rates: $49 to $79, Sunday–Thursday;
$79 to $99, Friday & Saturday

At night you can't miss it. From the apex of the pyramid, a powerful beam of light reaches into the sky. Airline pilots tell you that on a clear night they've seen it from two hundred miles away at cruising altitude. On the ground, visitors gather under the palms after dark to watch the ice blue eyes of the sphinx in front of the pyramid. As laser beams shoot from the eyes, mysterious images float in the air, seemingly tangible for a moment before they disappear.

The inspiration for Luxor Las Vegas is the ancient Temple of Luxor on the River Nile, dedicated to the sun god, Amon-Re, and built some three thousand years ago at the command of the pharoah Amenhotep III. The theme is ancient Egyptian, but the experience inside this pyramid is definitely twenty-first century.

Luxor Las Vegas has features never dreamed of in the days of Amenhotep III. A kaleidoscope of high-tech games and rides, restaurants, and shops pays tribute to the pharoahs and to archaeologists who later uncovered their long-buried civilizations. The intention here is to suggest a vast archaeological dig, where mysteries of ancient Egypt are revealed as if recently excavated.

When you walk in the front entrance, you come face-to-face with a needle-shaped monument covered with hieroglyphs, a copy of an ancient obelisk discovered at the Temple of Karnak in Egypt's Valley of Kings. A few feet away, a couple of lifelike camels raise their automated heads and begin a conversation in recorded voices, a sample of what you can expect during your visit to Luxor.

Hotel rooms on thirty floors surround a huge central atrium, but you hardly notice the quiet corridors leading away from crowds and colored lights in the center. Most visitors head straight for one of the three entertainment areas. You enter the pyramid in the middle, at the casino level, but it isn't absolutely necessary to navigate a jungle of slot machines on your way to other amusements. Escalators will carry you down to the arena level for a tour of **King Tut's Tomb** or showtime in **Pharoah's Theater**.

More escalators carry you up to the attraction level, where you find the interactive games and simulated-motion rides. Ticket booths surround a giant obelisk from which laser-light beams are projected into the upper atrium.

Attractions of the Past, Present, and Future

Secrets of the Luxor Pyramid

This main attraction is a three-part adventure created by Douglas Trumbull, the Hollywood special-effects artist who introduced us to other worlds in such films as

2001: A Space Odyssey and *Close Encounters of the Third Kind.* He also designed "Back to the Future—The Ride" at Universal Studios.

Each episode of the Luxor adventure is a separate show or ride. You can buy tickets individually or save a dollar by purchasing all three at once. Save more with an All-Attraction Pass, which also covers the **Nile River Tour** and admission to **King Tut's Tomb.** Prices can change, but the current cost of the comprehensive pass at the time of this book's publication is $15. Individual ticket prices are listed below. A telephone call is a good idea if you want current information. The Luxor number is (800) 288-1000.

Since you probably won't have time for all these adventures in one day, you can choose one episode of **Secrets of the Luxor Pyramid** this time and come back later to see the rest. Here's what to expect when making a choice:

Episode 1: In Search of the Obelisk
Sunday–Thursday 9 A.M. to 11 P.M.
Friday & Saturday 9 A.M. to 11:30 P.M.
Individual ticket: $5

Outside the theater (Luxor's "high-impact motion simulator") you hear a convincing news report that a noted archaeologist has discovered a mysterious crystal obelisk buried under the Luxor. Inside, you descend to the work site in an open-sided industrial elevator. Suddenly, you're part of a team attempting to recover the obelisk from very sophisticated thieves, who lead you on a dizzying chase through outer space. Brace yourself! Your seat will pitch and toss as galactic scenery races past you on-screen.

Children must be at least 42 inches tall and weigh at least 40 pounds to ride this one; warnings are posted for expectant mothers and anyone who has problems with heart, back, or neck. But these adventurers are not turned away—a midlevel corridor leads them into the "motionless theater," which is also accessible to wheelchairs.

Episode 2: Luxor Live?
   Sunday–Thursday 10 A.M. to 11 P.M.
   Friday & Saturday 10 A.M. to 11:30 P.M.
   Individual ticket: $4

This is a live television talk show, and you're part of the studio audience. Special guests and topics change from time to time. It seems down-to-earth and sedate enough, until one of the guests gets into a heated argument with the host. What happens? Just try to explain those elusive images that float before your eyes. Parents are warned that very young children may be frightened by dark sequences and loud sounds, but little ones, age three and younger, are admitted free if they sit on your lap.

Episode 3: Theater of Time
   Sunday–Thursday 10 A.M. to 11 P.M.
   Friday & Saturday 10 A.M. to 11:30 P.M.
   Individual ticket: $4

The story of the mysterious obelisk continues with some of the same characters as Episode 1. A cosmic time machine takes you into the future to the end of the world. A seven-story-high movie screen makes the most of three-dimensional computer imagery. No lap-sitting is allowed in the time machine, and parents are warned, once again, that toddlers may be frightened by the noise.

Nile River Tour

Every day 9 A.M. to 12:30 A.M.
Individual ticket: $3

Some newcomers begin their tour of the Luxor with a cruise on the "River Nile," a canal encircling the interior perimeter of the big pyramid on the main level. River-pilot guides keep up a lively commentary as they steer you past wall murals depicting ancient Egyptian life and tell you what to expect inside the Luxor resort. Other visitors save the restful river trip until later, when they're tired after a day of exploring shows, shops, games, and exhibits.

King Tut's Tomb and Museum

Every day 9 A.M. to 11 P.M.
Individual ticket: $3

If you want to start with history, take an escalator down to the arena level and tour this mini-museum. Recorded commentary guides you through as you stop at each exhibit, and your speaker-wand picks up the appropriate message.

The "tomb" is a replica of the treasure-filled burial place of the young Egyptian king Tutankhamen, discovered in 1922 by a British archaeologist named Howard Carter. At the time, the discovery made international headlines. No other pharoah's sepulchre in Egypt's Valley of Kings had been found intact. Others had been destroyed or looted long ago.

But Carter's persistent twenty-year quest led him down a long-hidden staircase to a suite of underground chambers that had been undisturbed for centuries. One of these rooms contained the mummified body of Tutankhamen, the "boy king," surrounded by the remains of everything he was expected to need in the afterlife. In other rooms, Carter discovered a storehouse of other objects provided for the dead king.

At Luxor Las Vegas, some five hundred objects displayed behind glass are reproductions of Tutankhamen's burial treasures. The originals are scattered around the world in museums in Cairo, New York, London, and Paris. Carter also uncovered a golden throne inlaid with colored glass, a broken chariot, boxes of preserved food, bunches of dried flowers, rolls of linen, jewelry, vases, statues, several beds, and an armless figure of a young man wearing a royal headdress. Many of these things have been duplicated for the Luxor museum display. Copies and adaptations of some of the treasures are for sale in Luxor shops.

According to Luxor brochures, the measurements of the tomb-museum are precise copies of the original excavated chambers. The only alteration was the removal of the descending stairway that led Carter underground.

Back to the Future— VirtuaLand and AS1

If your children loved the simulated-motion theaters, they'll be clamoring to go back to the attraction level to explore interactive games at **VirtuaLand**, "arcade of the future." Three-dimensional interactive games invite you test your skill and indulge your fantasies about race cars and fighter planes. The centerpiece is **AS1**, a simulated-motion theater with a 3-D Michael Jackson leading the adventure. In another game, you sit in your own race car and compete against seven other racers to capture the checkered-flag trophy. In case you have a hard time prying young gamesters out of VirtuaLand, maybe hunger pangs will help.

Getting Hungry?

The neon-lit **Millennium** restaurant allows you to remain in the future for a while as you order an "astro appetizer," a "cosmic quesadilla," or a "hyper-space salad." Ordinary dishes such as hamburgers and pizza are also on the menu, along with fruit smoothies and other healthful items. Gaze up through an open ceiling to the apex of the atrium. **Swensen's** ice-cream shop is adjacent.

If a glimpse of the New York City skyline brings you back to the present, the aroma of food will lead you straight to the **Manhattan Buffet**. Open for breakfast, lunch, and dinner, this spacious open-air buffet is set in the middle of a New York cityscape, where tables are clustered in a series of dining areas with different city themes. You may find yourself seated in a neighborhood diner or at a sidewalk cafe. On the buffet, you'll find old favorites such as roast beef and omelettes as well as lowfat dishes, international specialties, a big salad bar, and lots of desserts.

On the other side of the attraction level, next to the Luxor Live studio, you'll find **Papyrus**, open only at dinnertime. Although it sounds Egyptian, the ambience and food in this restaurant are Polynesian and Oriental, with palms, thatched-roof booths, and tropical decor. Dishes are Cantonese, Szechwan, and Pacific Rim. Reservations are recommended. Call (702) 262-4774. **Tut's Hut**, a tropical cocktail bar, is adjacent.

Down on the casino level, the **Pyramid Cafe** overlooks the River Nile and is open around-the-clock for breakfast, lunch, and dinner. Freshly baked breads and pastries are a specialty.

The **Nile Deli** opens out to the River Nile, but the theme is strictly downtown New York, with a traditional kosher-style delicatessen menu.

In the mood for fine dining? A special elevator takes you from the casino level to Luxor's two gourmet restaurants, hidden away on their own mezzanine. For fresh seafood, try the **Sacred Sea Room**. Prices here are a bit higher than at other Luxor restaurants, but you'll welcome the quiet, relaxed atmosphere after a whirlwind day of rides and sight-seeing. The menu changes daily to offer the freshest catch, and steaks and poultry are available for nonconformists. Call (702) 262-4772 for dinner reservations.

If you're ready to splurge, make a reservation at **Isis**, Luxor's elegant premier restaurant, where a French chef tempts your palate with imaginative dishes. Dine under a star-studded ceiling, surrounded by reminders of Egypt's past. For reservations, call (702) 262-4773.

A Little Shopping?

No problem—shops are located strategically on every level. Along with other souvenirs and necessities, Luxor shops offer books, prints, and replicas of Egyptian artifacts.

Sobek's Sundries is the place to find a newspaper, toothpaste, aspirin, or postcards. Candy and cosmetics, too.

The Source provides reproductions of jewelry, paintings, and pottery found in King Tut's tomb. For a price, you can even buy small authenticated Egyptian antiquities.

Innerspace, on the casino level, is another gallery of limited-edition reproductions. You'll also find jewelry and resort clothes.

The Scarab Shop and **Park Avenue Shop** on the attraction level feature T-shirts and souvenirs with the

Luxor logo. There's more jewelry, too, including some exclusive sterling silver designs.

If You're Staying at the Luxor . . .

Take an elevator to your room and, for a moment, you may think you've wandered onto one of the rides in the amusement atrium. All elevators climb the slanting sides of the pyramid at a 39-degree angle, like a very smooth ski lift. Banks of elevators are located at each of the pyramid's four corners, so be sure to remember which one will take you to your floor. Luxor has 2,562 rooms and suites.

Open the door of your room, and kids will run to the slanting windows for a look at picture-postcard views of mountains or city glitter. The Egyptian motif turns up everywhere in the decor, including the boxed soaps in the bathroom, a favorite with children.

Room prices change, but the recent standard has been $49 to $79, Sunday through Thursday, and $79 to $99, Friday and Saturday. Luxury suites are more expensive. Children twelve and younger stay free.

Between excursions, a nap is restful—but an hour in the health spa will do wonders for any frazzled parent. At Luxor's spa, you'll find steam rooms, saunas, and indoor jacuzzis. Pamper yourself with a facial or a massage. For serious workouts, there's a weight room with treadmills, exercycles, and a professional trainer to supervise the effort. If it fits your schedule, sign up for a water aerobics class, or do your own water workout with the whole family in Luxor's outdoor pool. Spa and pool are accessible from a ramp at the casino level at the west entrance. Hours vary with the season, so dial 4366 for information (outside the hotel, call 262-4366).

WALK THROUGH TIME
TO CAMELOT

A very different world—a medieval realm of knights and
ladies, minstrels and jugglers—is just a short walk from
the north entrance of Luxor, on the southwest corner of
Tropicana Avenue and the Strip. Excalibur, opened in
1990, was the first of the new Las Vegas theme resorts
created for Circus Circus Enterprises.

Excalibur Hotel & Casino
3850 Las Vegas Boulevard South
Las Vegas, NV 89109-4300
Room reservations: (800) 937-7777
Inside Nevada: (702) 597-7700
Fax: (702) 597-7009
Rates: children under 18 stay free;
from $39 per night Sunday–Thursday;
$79 to $89 Friday & Saturday

Step into a cobblestone courtyard and enter the rock-
walled foyer of a fairy-tale castle. When sunlight filters
through the leaded stained-glass windows, patches of
colored light brighten the entrance. Straight ahead,
slot machines and gaming tables remind you that this
is a modern-day casino, but kids instinctively head for
the **Wizard's Arcade** or **Merlin's Magic Motion
Machines** on the Fantasy Faire level below.

To ease yourselves through the time warp, you may
want to start on the upper level with a stroll through

the **Medieval Village**. In the middle of the village, free ten-minute shows are presented daily on the Court Jester's Stage, every half hour from 10 A.M. to 10 P.M. Street musicians, jugglers, and magicians give impromptu performances at street corners among the shops and restaurants.

Getting Hungry?

Expect a few anachronisms in the Medieval Village. For a taste of the Old West, there's **Wild Bill's Saloon and Steakhouse** with its live country music. You'll also find **Lance-A-Lotta-Pasta**, serving Italian dishes at lunch and dinner.

In other parts of the castle, the **Round Table Buffet** serves breakfast, lunch, and dinner at moderate prices. **The Sherwood Forest Cafe** is open twenty-four hours a day and features a children's menu for small visitors.

Two more restaurants are open for dinner only. **Sir Galahad's** is a Tudor-style prime rib room, and **Camelot** is a romantic castle chamber serving gourmet dishes by candlelight.

King Arthur's Tournament

This is the centerpiece of an evening at Excalibur. In a nine-hundred-seat arena on the Fantasy Faire level, armored knights on horseback test their skill in combat with sword and lance as the audience cheers. Dinner is served, medieval-style, while you watch the jousting. Drink soup from a pewter bowl and eat roast fowl with your fingers as Merlin the Magician appears in the arena and introduces the show.

It's a spectacle with a story. A lone youth on horseback gallops fast around the arena and stops to rest in a corner of the English countryside. As he sleeps, Merlin transforms the young man into Jeffrey, the White Knight, hero of the evening. In his dream, Jeffrey is a knight of the Round Table, competing in an elaborate tournament staged in the presence of King Arthur and Queen Guinevere.

Dignitaries from all parts of the realm are seated beneath banners of their regions—and you are among them. Cheer your own knight as he battles his opponent, then join a wedding celebration when Jeffrey wins the hand of a princess. You'll see acrobats and tumblers, dancing girls and circus riders before the show ends. When Merlin swirls his midnight blue cape and waves his wand, the whole scene dissolves in a magic mist.

As Las Vegas dinner shows go, this one's a bargain at $29.95 per person, which includes the three-course dinner, taxes, and tips. That's a hefty price for a family of four, but if you're prepared for such prices it won't shock you too much.

A Nebraska couple with five children attended the show last year and pronounced it their favorite attraction in Las Vegas. Even the thirteen-month-old baby was enchanted.

King Arthur's Tournament is staged twice nightly, at 6 and 8:30 P.M., and reservations are necessary. The earlier show is especially popular, so it's a good idea to plan ahead, up to five days in advance, by calling (702) 597-7600.

Merlin and the Dragon

Outside Excalibur, crowds gather at the castle moat after dark to see Merlin the Magician's own show. Changing colored lights, reflected in the water, are a signal that something is about to happen. Suddenly, from a cavern beneath the moat, a fifty-one-foot dragon emerges, exhaling flames as he slowly undulates toward Merlin's tower. A robotic Merlin comes out on the rampart and announces his intention to slay this dragon to restore peace in the countryside. And so he does . . . every hour on the hour, from 8 P.M. to 1 A.M. nightly, depending upon weather conditions. You can't beat the price of this show—it's free.

Merlin's Playground

Back inside the castle on the Fantasy Faire level, you'll find carnival games and **Merlin's Magic Motion Machines** anytime from 9 A.M. until after midnight. If you've been to Luxor and the MGM, you've already experienced one or two simulated-motion rides, but Excalibur introduced them to North America before the newer resorts were built. Merlin's pair of forty-eight-seat theaters offer five different adventures at $2.50 per ride.

Space Race Directed by *Star Wars* creator George Lucas, this ride takes you on a breathless chase through the cosmos and into a battle with alien foes.

The Devil's Mine This is a wild and unpredictable ride through underground tunnels and caverns.

Desert Duel Is that a chasm ahead? This ride carries you in a bouncing jeep through unexpected hazards over rocky dirt trails. Where are the brakes?

The Revolution This dizzying roller coaster is borrowed from "Magic Mountain" in Disneyland.

Runaway Train This train races through steep mountain passes and tunnels—with no brakes.

All this frantic movement is accomplished through the magic of seventy-millimeter film, five-channel stereo sound, and specially designed seats that pitch and shake, synchronized with the action on-screen.

A Show for Dog Lovers

If your children are too young for an evening performance of King Arthur's Tournament, consider Excalibur's afternoon show.

Sooper Dogs, a crowd-pleaser for pet lovers, features a changing cast of canine performers. Young audiences cheer the antics of "Moore's Mess o' Mutts," a comedy troupe of trick dogs rescued from dog pounds and Humane Society shelters by their trainer, Stacy Moore. The pups climb ladders, jump through hoops, and obey— or ignore—Moore's commands.

Another Sooper Dogs headliner is Scooter, team mascot for the San Francisco 49ers and "world champion frisbee-catching dog," with his trainer, Lou Mack.

Showtime is 2 P.M. on weekdays except Wednesday, the dogs' day off. The dogs perform twice on Saturday and Sunday, at noon and 2 P.M. Tickets are $4.95, tax included, up to three days in advance or on performance day at Excalibur ticket booths.

If You're Staying at the Castle . . .

Excalibur may be the best bargain of the new mega-resorts on the Las Vegas Strip. Prices change from time to time, but a family of four can get a room for as little as $39 per night, Sunday through Thursday. The rate is always higher on weekends, holidays, and during conventions. There's plenty of room for you and a lot of other vacationers, with 4,032 rooms in the four 28-story towers.

All standard rooms have two queen-sized beds or one king-size, with medieval decor in shades of red or blue. Bathrooms have showers but no tubs, except for a few deluxe suites with jacuzzis. These are priced from $135 a night and up. Some standard rooms are designed for disabled travelers, with handrails in the bathrooms. All public areas have ramps for wheelchair access.

While you're a resident of the realm, you'll want to save time for splashing in one of Excalibur's two swimming pools. The semicircular main pool, 120 feet across at its widest point, is separated from the rear pool by a twenty-foot artificial rock formation complete with waterfalls and pine trees. Water slides are built into the rock face. Both pools are equipped with mobile hoists to assist disabled guests, and ramps provide easy wheelchair access to snack bar and towel station.

MOVING ON . . .

Beyond Excalibur's castle walls, the rest of Las Vegas waits to be explored. Walk across the strip to begin another adventure.

CHAPTER 3

The MGM Grand

From Excalibur's portcullis, you have a clear view of two more huge resorts on the other side of the Strip. The Tropicana, behind landscaped gardens directly across Las Vegas Boulevard, has been here long enough to give its name to the cross street, Tropicana Avenue. Swimming pools with waterfalls and a collection of colorful tropical birds make the Tropicana Resort worth including in a family's sightseeing itinerary, but right now your kids want to explore the MGM Grand with its Grand Adventures theme park. They've heard it compared to Disneyland.

On the northeast corner of the Strip at Tropicana Avenue, a giant golden lion crouches at the main entrance to the MGM Grand. Behind this colossal trademark, a complex of emerald green glass contains more than five thousand hotel rooms and suites. The adjacent MGM Grand Garden has movable walls, easily converting a convention center and exhibition hall into a sports arena or concert hall with 15,222 seats. More theaters are inside the casino and in the thirty-three-acre theme park out back. Then there are tennis courts, a swimming complex, and a health club and spa. The whole MGM property covers 112 acres. When it opened at the end of 1993, the MGM Grand set a record as the world's largest hotel, casino, and theme park.

Getting there on foot is a small adventure in itself. If you're starting from the other side of the Strip, eight lanes of traffic come between you and your destination. Traffic lights control the flow, but cars turning onto the Strip from Tropicana Avenue can slow you down or take you by surprise. At this busy crossroads, overhead walkways are your best bet. They're easy to reach by escalators, elevators, or stairways at each corner. One pedestrian overpass leads from Excalibur to the Tropicana, another from the Tropicana to the MGM Grand.

Arriving by car is simple. The self-parking garage has space for 4,800 cars, and parking valets have another 1,200 spaces tucked away in an underground lot. Clearly marked driveways and ramps make it easy to find your way into the garage. On a busy weekend, you may spend a few minutes searching for an empty space, but once you've parked you'll find plenty of signs and arrows to point you in the right direction. A broad passageway leads straight to the registration lobby.

The MGM Grand
3799 Las Vegas Boulevard
Las Vegas, NV 89109
Room reservations: (800) 929-1111
Inside Nevada: (702) 891-7777
Fax: (702) 891-3036
Rates: from $69; call for specifics

Whether you're staying in the hotel or planning to make the MGM just one of many attractions on your sightseeing list, you'll find yourself wishing for more time. Allow at least an entire morning or afternoon for this visit. You'll wish you had all day . . . or longer.

THE EMERALD CITY

From the sidewalk, follow the Yellow Brick Road through the front door, between the two massive paws of the eight-foot-tall lion, and you're transported to the Land of Oz. Beyond the white picket fence of the Kansas garden (where Dorothy lived with Auntie Em before a tornado carried her to Oz), you see the gates of the Emerald City—a seven-story representation of the magical capital of Oz. Figures of Dorothy and Toto are there to greet you, along with the Cowardly Lion, the Scarecrow, and the Tin Woodsman—all looking very much as they appeared in the classic MGM film, *The Wizard of Oz*.

From time to time, the indoor sky above the Emerald City darkens, and the sound of a storm is heralded by flashes of lightning. As the storm grows louder (Is it a tornado?) you see the figure of a witch on a broomstick flying across the sky. Through it all, you hear the voices of Dorothy and her friends . . . and the cackling of the Wicked Witch of the West. Once the storm has passed, stars emerge from the clouds and shine until they're chased away by a pink dawn. This spectacle is repeated continually all day, every day, for anyone who walks through the door.

Inside the Emerald City, there's a small theater where **The Wizard's Secret** magic show is scheduled at regular intervals. Precise times are posted at the

Emerald City box office, and you can buy tickets in advance. Before showtime, you'll be ushered through a gate in the picket fence for a stroll along a winding path in Auntie Em's garden as well as for closer encounters with Oz characters before the Wizard himself shows you some of his magic tricks.

Be warned: Some of the special effects may be too scary for small children. *You* know it's just an illusion when the prisoner loses his head on the guillotine, but it looks awfully convincing in the theater. One young mother told us that her three-year-old daughter hid her face during some parts of the performance.

But we've only begun to explore. This place is huge— No wonder they call it "Grand"!

A gaming space bigger than Yankee Stadium is divided into four casinos with separate themes: Hollywood, Emerald City, Monte Carlo, and Sports. Without a guide, expect to get lost several times; you'll wander past showrooms, shops, restaurants, and bar/lounges. Casino areas are filled with adult games and slot machines, but children will follow their own special radar to the theme park.

A passageway like a bustling city street leads from the casino toward the park. Along the way, more restaurants tempt you to stop for a snack or a meal. The **Wizard's Midway & Arcade** invites kids of all ages to come in and challenge the video machines or compete for prizes in carnival games.

Near the theme park gates, a giant toy soldier guards the entrance to **MGM Grand Youth Center**, a "youth hotel" offering supervised activities for children ages three to twelve and excursions for youngsters three to sixteen. The youth center is discussed later in this chapter.

On a first visit to the MGM Grand, most families with kids arrive with an immediate destination in mind.

MGM GRAND ADVENTURES THEME PARK

Behind the casino complex, kids will discover their number one reason for coming to the MGM Grand in the first place. If they like Disneyland, they'll love this smaller theme park, the first of its kind in Las Vegas. Family members can choose among action rides, simulated-motion theaters, arcades, shops, restaurants, and movie-set replicas of exotic street scenes around the world.

You never know who's going to turn up in this adventureland. Actors dressed as Popeye, Olive Oyl, Betty Boop, Tumbleweed, and other MGM cartoon characters roam through the park, greeting visitors. Dorothy and her friends from Oz may pass you on the street. King L. J., the MGM lion/ambassador, often brings his own family to talk with children and pose for snapshots. Entertainers give impromptu free performances on the streets of New York, London, New Orleans, or Tumbleweed Gulch.

Most of this happens outdoors, so remember to prepare for the weather. On sunny winter days it's heaven, but summers can be blistering hot, in which case you'll spend more time inside air-conditioned rides and theaters. Whatever the season, be sure to wear comfortable shoes—you'll walk a lot.

Ticket prices have changed several times since the park opened, so it's a good idea to check by phone before you go; call (702) 891-7979. Ordinarily, admission to the park is free. You can walk in and stroll around anywhere outside the rides and shows. For those attractions, you'll need an all-day pass. The current price for a one-day pass is $15 for adults, $10 for children 12 and younger, allowing you unlimited access to all the shows and rides you can cram into a single day. Prices go up in the summer (May 27 through September 5) to $16.95 for adults, $13.95 for children 12 and younger.

When you buy your pass, you'll be given a map of the park. Hold on to it. You may need it, especially if family members become separated from each other. If anybody goes off alone, pick a spot on the map and agree to meet there at a given time. Small children should stick with parents.

Any Questions?

If you need a stroller or wheelchair, stop at Guest Services, immediately inside the park entrance. Here's where you'll find emergency supplies for babies—disposable diapers and the like—and coin-operated lockers for storing packages, jackets, or anything else you don't want to carry around all day. And in case you or your children lose something as you wander, the lost-and-found desk is part of Guest Services. The MGM Grand Adventures Rangers are security people who will answer your questions, help you find medical attention if you need it, or direct you to the First Aid Center on Asian Street. Be sure to point them out to your small children at the start of the day; if the kids get lost or separated, a Ranger can help you and your children find your way back to each other.

Walk through Casablanca Plaza, out the gate with its distinctive minarets, and suddenly you're on New York Street at the edge of Central Park. After that, find your way through the Asian Village to French Street, the Salem Waterfront, Tumbleweed Gulch, New Orleans Street, Olde England Street, and the Rio Grande Cantina.

Along the way, you'll want to sample a few rides, arcades, restaurants, and shops. Some of the thrill rides are not recommended for small children, so you'll find height requirements posted at each attraction.

An Adventurous Menu of Rides

Lightning Bolt   This one's short but scary. It's a breathless indoor roller-coaster ride through outer space, ending with a simulated night landing over Las Vegas. When it's over, you'll find a photo of your own terrified face among a gallery of snapshots taken by hidden cameras during the ride. (To destroy the evidence, buy one.)

Backlot River Tour   At first glance, it seems to be a calm, lazy, river-barge tour of a movie set, but wait till you find yourself in the middle of a war movie! It wouldn't be fair to give away all the surprises. Just be prepared for a jolt or two.

Deep Earth Exploration   On a geological expedition to the center of the earth, you travel aboard Gopher I. It's a motion simulator so convincing you'll think you've made a quick descent in a fast elevator. Watch out for boiling lava from that erupting volcano! It's easy to forget it's just on movie film.

Grand Canyon Rapids   Expect to get a bit wet while racing through white-water rapids in a big nine-passenger inflatable raft. Just when you think you've hit calm water, after surviving Wilderness Rapids and Flash Flood Gulch . . . well, see for yourself!

Parisian Taxis   These are fun if you like those little bumper cars at carnivals. Pretend you're in a Paris traffic jam and brace yourself for a few collisions.

The Haunted Mine   Cursed by an old Indian chief, so the story goes, this spooky old abandoned mine is still haunted by the chief's restless spirit.

Over the Edge   Visit a quaint old sawmill in a Great Northwest timber forest and hold on to your kids. It's another roller coaster with some steep drops.

Four Theaters

Manhattan Theater   Sit down and rest your feet in this 650-seat auditorium. The program changes from time to time, but it could be the Peking Circus, a troupe of China's most gifted tumblers, contortionists and more, presenting a mind-boggling, visually exciting show.

Pirate's Cove, featuring Dueling Pirates   In an outdoor stadium, a band of likable mutineers takes over a pirate ship as masts break, towers explode, and hungry sharks lurk in the water. Join the crowd and cheer the gymnastic stunts of your favorite pirates.

You're in the Movies!   So you've dreamed of playing the hero in a western adventure—or the romantic lead in a love story? Some of those daydreams just might come true, for a few minutes anyway, in this movie studio. Members of the audience are chosen, costumed, and given scripts. Then their performances are electronically combined with existing film. (Hey, look at the screen! Is that you up there?)

Magic Screen Theater   More movies, but this time you don't perform. The entertainment schedule changes, but past programs have featured *Rock Around the Clock* and *The Three Stooges,* reminding old-timers of those Saturday matinee double-features at the neighborhood movie house.

A Place to Relax

Rio Grande Cantina   In good weather (almost year-round), you can sit in this outdoor garden cafe in Tumble-weed Gulch and listen to live music and entertainment. To reserve a section of the Cantina for a birthday party or other celebration, call (702) 891-7922.

Three Arcades

Somebody in your family is sure to spot one of these carnival-style booths. All three invite you to test your steady aim or pitching skills. In Tumbleweed Gulch, win a stuffed animal at the **Shooting Gallery** or simply prove your superiority with electronic games at **Quick Draw.** If you can toss a ring with precision, capture another prize at **Les Boats** on French Street.

When You're Hungry . . .

Fancier restaurants are inside the casino, but you can find a nourishing meal, fast food, cold drinks, or a quick cup of coffee without leaving the adventure park. Take your pick:

Burger King   Familiar fast food: hamburgers, fries, and Pepsi. Also chicken sandwiches and a few low-cal items.

Nathan's Famous   The atmosphere is Coney Island circa 1916, with an updated menu. How about an all-beef hot dog with salad and fresh lemonade? Or maybe chicken with fries?

The Cotton Blossom Arcade & Snack Bar   Board a paddle-wheel riverboat anchored in the bayou; order snacks, soft drinks, and beer and wine. An arcade is surrounded with the ambiance of the French Quarter on New Orleans Street.

Mama Ilardo's Pizzeria   Choose from a list of pizzas and other Italian specialties and relax while you watch the passing crowds on French Street.

Hamada Orient Express   Hungry for Chinese-style beef and chicken dishes? Also available are rice, egg rolls, seafood, and tea. A fortune cookie predicts: "You will travel far . . ."

Kenny Rogers' Roasters   Chicken roasting over an open wood fire sends a tempting aroma across the Salem Waterfront. It also makes a hefty meal when you add side dishes and desserts.

Trolly Treats   Cold lemonade when you're thirsty or a candy bar for quick energy are on the list of snacks available from this cart on New York Street.

Benninger's Gourmet Coffees   Time for a quiet break before moving on to another show. Coffee and pastries fill the bill. Even caffeine-free dieters find temptations here.

Hildegard's Ice Cream Parlor   Stepping out of the Tumbleweed comic strip, Hildegard's serves frozen goodies, candies, and sandwiches. Watch out for that sweet tooth, but if it gets the best of you, here's the place to satisfy it.

What Shall We Take to the Folks Back Home?

A dozen shops scattered through the park will remind you that you really do want to find a gift for Grandma or Uncle Ed or the neighbor who's feeding your cats. When there's time to browse between rides and shows, wander into a shop or two. The map will help you locate the kind of store you're looking for.

Out of film? Check the **Kodak Photo Center** near the main gate. They'll also process your film in just two hours. You'll find disposable cameras and blank video-tapes here, too. Next door at the **Photoplay Gallery**, you can see a portrait of yourself on the cover of a national magazine—and take home "proof" of your fame.

Children may forget all about budgeting their spending money when they see the dolls, trains, masks, and gadgets at **Bayou Toys.** This could be hard on your resolve (or your wallet), but some mementos are inexpensive.

Keepsakes and T-shirts at the **Casablanca General Store** will remind you of favorite movie characters. You'll find more MGM souvenirs at **Backstage Collectibles** on New York Street and **Studio Souvenirs** in Casablanca Plaza.

At **Backlot Heirlooms** on French Street, you'll find more collectibles: limited-edition prints, plates, dolls, and figurines. **Hollywood Clothiers** offers wearable movie mementos, including shirts, scarves, and jewelry.

Artisans demonstrate their skills at **Behind the Scenes Craft Co.** on Olde England Street. You can watch them at work as they create designs in leather, wood, pottery, and glass.

At the **Old West Supply Company** in Tumbleweed Gulch, there's no telling what might have arrived on the latest stagecoach. Souvenirs? Bet on it! At **Grand Gestures** you'll find the finest international gift brands, floral services, custom gift baskets, and tuxedo rentals.

In case you must communicate with the outside world, public telephones throughout the park are easy to locate on your map. You'll find restrooms and diaper stations in the same locations. If your cash supply is running low, there's an automatic teller machine on Olde England Street.

OTHER MGM FEATURES

Activity Daycare for Kids

Provided they're at least three years old and potty-trained, children can be VIP guests at hourly rates from 8 A.M. to midnight in the **MGM Grand Youth Center**, located near the theme park. When parents or kids want a few hours of nontogetherness, the trained counselors are available to supervise games and activities in the center. Counselors also conduct tours of the park for children ages six to sixteen. Check in at the center's registration desk (inside the glass doors, across from the 30,000-square-foot **Oz Midway and Arcade**) to find out what's on the current schedule.

On a typical day, you'll find an assortment of three- to twelve-year-old children (Director Mike Messner calls them "Munchkins") at play in the center's four separate rooms. Younger kids, ages three to six, stay busy with arts and crafts, blocks and puzzles, dollhouses, and tumbling mats.

The Game Room, for seven to twelve year olds, has Ping-Pong and Super Nintendo Air Hockey. Chess, anyone? In the Arts and Crafts Room, young artists can express their creativity with fingerpaints and watercolors, and the multi-purpose room features basketball, floor hockey, and dodge ball. While their children are meeting other kids at the Youth Center, parents can carry a beeper to keep in touch. If a young child is a little nervous in unfamiliar surroundings, counselers can call parents anytime. For hotel guests, the charge per child is $5 an hour for up to five hours. After that, children must return to their parents for at least two hours before coming back to the center for another five-hour maximum. This schedule is strictly enforced. If a child is left longer than five hours, parents are charged an extra $50 per hour. After midnight, the same penalty applies.

The MGM Grand Youth Activity Center has its own snack bar. Breakfast is served at 9 A.M. for $3, lunch at 1 P.M. for $4, and dinner at 7 P.M. for $5.

Excursions for Kids and Teens

Teenagers aren't included in the Youth Center activities, but they have their own special pursuits. Excursions for six to sixteen year olds are more ambitious opportunities to meet other children and teens from around the world. Ask for information at the registration desk, or call extension 3200 from your hotel room.

The Grand Adventures Theme Park Excursion is an all-day expedition with counselors who know the history of the park and can answer questions about behind-the-scenes operations. The $70 package includes a six-hour tour, entrance fees and taxes, rides and shows within the park, lunch and a snack, a T-shirt, and a surprise gift. If you're treating more than one child to the tour, the charge is $70 for the first child and $60 for each sibling. Reservations and payments must be made at the Youth Center reservation desk by 6 P.M. on the day before the scheduled excursion.

Beach Parties

Cool Pool Parties for the six-to-sixteen crowd are supervised by lifeguard/counselors at the sandy beach beside the MGM pool. Swimming, beach games, snacks, and a T-shirt are included in the $25 price. Pool gatherings are usually organized on Saturdays, Sundays, and Wednesdays from 1:30 to 4:30 P.M. Ask for a current schedule at the Youth Center reservation desk.

Baby-sitting Options

While the kids are having fun with contemporaries, you and your spouse can make independent plans. A night on the town? A game of tennis? Shopping? A beauty treatment at the Grand Spa? The possibilities are limitless.

If your children are younger than three or are not yet potty-trained, there are options besides the Youth Activity Center. Advisers at the registration desk can provide a list of qualified baby-sitting services, with telephone numbers and prices. A sitter in your hotel room is something to consider if you'd like to enjoy a quiet dinner for two without pushing a stroller.

SO MANY RESTAURANTS...
SO LITTLE TIME

Plan ahead and make a reservation, or just stroll along restaurant row and read the menus before making up your mind. In the mood for seafood? Get a table at the **Cracked Crab.** Have a yen for Chinese dishes in a quiet, exotic setting? Pass through the ornate gates of **Dragon Court.** Or maybe you'd prefer the hearty, Old English food and decor at **Sir Reginald's Steakhouse.**

Wolfgang Puck's Pizza is a casual California favorite, and **Pinocchio's** is the place to go when the family longs for pasta.

Gourmet cuisine with a southwestern flavor is the star attraction at the **Coyote Cafe**, restaurateur Mark Miller's Las Vegas version of his original Coyote restaurant in Santa Fe. (Maybe you've seen *Miller's Coyote Cafe Cookbook* or *The Great Chile Book* or perhaps the new *Coyote's Pantry.*) The MGM Coyote Cafe has two sections, a casual all-day-and-late-night cafe and a candlelit dining room open only for dinner. The place is popular. To save yourself a long wait for a table, make advance reservations for dinner.

When the whole family is together, you can't beat the **Oz Buffet** for breakfast, lunch, or dinner. It's inside the casino, in the Emerald City area. Don't be surprised or discouraged if you see a long line of hungry tourists waiting for tables—the place is huge and the line moves fast. Service is efficient and the food is excellent. Carry your own tray.

Inside the Hollywood casino area, the **Studio Cafe** is a twenty-four-hour coffee shop with table service.

If fast food is what you're after, go back to the Midway and stop at **One Liners Food Court**, a cluster of vending stalls surrounding a central patio full of tables. Pick your familiar favorites from McDonald's, Taco Bell, Nathan's, and Hamada Express.

SHOPPING IN THE HOTEL

If you didn't have time to browse in the theme park boutiques, or even if you did, you're not likely to leave the MGM Grand without visiting at least one of the shops inside the hotel.

MGM Grand & Co., across from the registration desk, is the hotel's largest retail store, open around-the-clock. Looking for sunglasses? Cosmetics? Souvenirs? You'll find them here, along with luggage, resort clothes, and leather jackets.

Emerald City Gift Shop, across from the Oz Buffet, displays all sorts of Wizard of Oz merchandise, from Dorothy dolls to pewter figurines of Oz characters. You can buy film for your camera here and also get two-hour film processing.

MGM Grand Adventures Store on the Midway is open twenty-four hours, rounding up a collection of souvenirs from the theme park for last-minute shoppers.

The Front Page, open around-the-clock near hotel elevators, is an indispensible source of newspapers, books, magazines, snacks, toothpaste, and shaving cream.

If You're Staying at the MGM . . .

A room at the MGM Grand makes it easy for families to take restful breaks between excursions into the theme park. With so many things to see and do under one roof (and in the big backyard) you could spend days at this resort without venturing beyond its borders.

Somewhere among the MGM's 5,005 rooms (including 744 suites) you'll find your own refuge from the crowds. One of ninety-three hotel elevators will take you to your floor. In the room, movie star portraits on the walls suggest a decorating theme from *Gone With the Wind* or *The Wizard of Oz* or perhaps *Casablanca*. Marble baths convey Hollywood luxury; soaps and shampoos are generous.

Room prices may surprise you—they're definitely not the highest in town. The recent range for MGM standard rooms has been from $69 to $189, but there's too much variation to be sure of a price without phoning first. Better still, ask your travel agent about package arrangements that include airfare. You may discover a real bargain, depending on the time of year and how far you'll be traveling. Children under twelve stay free anytime.

MOVING ON . . .

The three enormous resorts explored so far offer enough entertainment to keep you busy for a week or more without moving beyond the intersection of Las Vegas Boulevard and Tropicana Avenue. But there's a whole lot more to see, so let's move on.

Travel north on the Strip, past glittering signs of older landmarks such as Aladdin, the Jockey Club, and Bally's. We're heading for Flamingo Road, where another fantasy adventure begins.

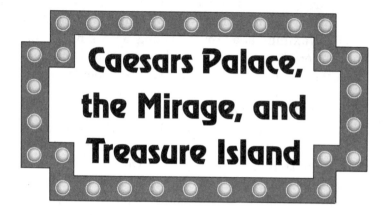

CHAPTER 4

Caesars Palace,
the Mirage, and
Treasure Island

Three self-contained worlds coexist in the long block between Flamingo and Spring Mountain Roads on the west side of the Strip. **Caesars Palace**, the **Mirage** and **Treasure Island**—each stirs the visitor's imagination with a separate set of fantasies woven around a distinctive theme.

CAESARS PALACE — A VEGAS INSTITUTION

Caesars Palace is the oldest tenant of this block, dominating the Flamingo crossroads since it opened in August 1966. At that time the palace seemed enormous, with 680 hotel rooms. In the Garden of the Gods swimming pool and spa, guests were as pampered as imperial Roman dignitaries. Lavish fountains and marble statues made Caesars Palace an international symbol of Las Vegas opulence. When Caesars Colosseum Convention Complex opened in September 1966, a gathering of National Milk Producers became the first business group

45

to mill around in the meeting rooms and twenty-five thousand square feet of exhibition space. At the same time, the Circus Maximus showroom opened with singer Andy Williams on stage, and the 980 seats were filled with fans. Since then, Caesars Palace has become a popular setting for moviemakers and television entertainment.

From the beginning, there was no apostrophe in *Caesars*. Founder Jay Sarno explained that this palace was not to be a monument to a single Caesar. All guests were to be treated as though *they* were Caesars. Now, nearly thirty years later, guests still receive the imperial treatment—often at imperial prices—with ever-increasing room to move around. More towers with more rooms have been added over the years, bringing the total number of rooms and suites to 1,514. Even in the face of competition from newer hotels with two or three times as many rooms, Caesars Palace has kept its reputation as a showplace and a top destination for conventions and vacations, attracting an estimated thirteen million visitors every year.

Caesars Palace
3570 Las Vegas Boulevard South
Las Vegas, NV 89109
General information: (702) 731-7110
Room reservations: (800) 634-6661
Inside Nevada: (702) 731-7222
Fax: (702) 731-6636
Rates: from $115 to $190; call for
specifics

You can't miss the entrance to Caesars. From the Strip, the first thing you notice is a row of fountains spraying columns of water as high as thirty-five feet in the air, splashing down into an oval-shaped pool. A huge reproduction of the winged *Victory at Samothrace* stands at the front end of the pool, looking as if it had been borrowed from the Louvre in Paris. Along the pool's sides, avenues of meticulously trimmed Italian cypresses lead toward a portico where more Greek and Roman statues stand between white columns flanking the main door.

Designed for adult tastes in the days when Las Vegas ignored the existence of families with children, Caesars hasn't rushed to add attractions especially for kids. But when visitors bring their families, Caesars is ready to entertain them. Just walking through the place is entertainment enough for browsers who appreciate Roman architecture and landscaping and the marble replicas of famous statues, including Michelangelo's *David*.

Sightseers pay nothing to ride Caesars "people movers," automated walkways leading from the Strip to Caesar's Palace and The Forum Shops. (More than a shopping mall, The Forum Shops at Caesars is a popular Las Vegas attraction for families with children. See chapter 7 for more information.) Another favorite with kids and their parents is **The World of Caesar** at the entrance to the central people mover. Inside an ornate rotunda, designed to resemble a Roman temple, you discover a miniature re-creation of Rome as it might have looked two thousand years ago.

Step onto the moving walkway and you're carried into this miniature ancient city, past scaled-down replicas of such historic landmarks as the Colosseum, the Forum, and Palatine Hill. Special effects deliver the sights and sounds of a Roman celebration going on inside one of the miniature buildings. Before leaving the rotunda, you'll meet Caesar and Cleopatra—small automated figures who allow you to peek inside their royal treasury. Still on the moving walkway, you travel above the Caesars Palace gardens to take in a view of the Las Vegas Strip on your way to the Olympic Casino.

Caesars people movers take you into the casino but they don't take you out. Once inside, you might ask what's showing at Caesars **Omnimax Theatre**. Maybe it's a travel film about an African safari, or an undersea visit with sharks, or a flight into space. This dome-shaped movie theater has a screen that surrounds you, making you part of the action. Reclining seats make it easy to see what's happening above and around you. Programs change regularly, but shows are scheduled every afternoon and evening: Sunday through Thursday, 2 to 10 P.M., and Friday and Saturday, 1 to 11 P.M. To plan ahead, phone (702) 731-7900.

Dining Caesars-Style

Some daytime sight-seers bring their families to Caesars restaurants, especially for spur-of-the-moment meals and snacks in **La Piazza Food Court**. Separate stations for Mexican, Asian, New York deli, and other specialites surround the court, where you carry your own tray to one of 225 tables and booths. You can drop in for a cup of coffee and fresh pastry, a glass of juice, or a full meal. Each item is priced separately, except for some combinations, and affordable prices are a pleasant surprise. You'll find continental breakfast available every day and a full breakfast on weekends. Late at night, **La Piazza** becomes a lounge with live music.

When you're really hungry, help yourself to the lavish displays at the **Palatium Buffet** for breakfast, lunch, or dinner. An elegant weekend brunch is a popular favorite. If you prefer table service, **Cafe Roma** is a comfortable spot for an informal meal, twenty-four hours a day.

To relax beside a waterfall in an Oriental garden, make a reservation at **Ah'So**, the Japanese steakhouse where dinner is cooked at your table. For a broad selection of fresh seafood and prime steaks, try **Nero's**.

For breakfast, lunch, or dinner with a view of the **Garden of the Gods** pool complex, settle into a fanback chair at **Primavera**. The house specialty is fresh pasta, and you'll find plenty of elegant alternatives. Sip an espresso or cappuccino and enjoy the scenery.

Several gourmet restaurants at Caesars Palace have won culinary awards. The **Palace Court** receives accolades for its American and continental haute cuisine. At the **Empress Court**, authentic Cantonese recipes impress the critics. And the **Bacchanal** serves up a seven-course feast in imperial style, with costumed waitresses pouring vintage wines. Be prepared to empty your wallet or strain a credit card.

Caesars Magical Empire, a brand-new entertainment and dining complex, is scheduled to open before the end of 1995. Announced plans include two theaters, a grotto, and "mystical performances" by magicians who promise to make spectators part of the show.

Go-for-Broke Accommodations

Hotel rooms at Caesars are expensive. A standard room with a king-sized bed or two double beds will cost at least $115 to $190 per night. Suites with one bedroom are available from $500 up, and two-bedroom suites start at $650. Add the 8 percent room tax and you're talking about a chunk of money. Forget about the fantasy suites with stars on the ceiling and jacuzzis in the bedrooms. Posted rates are $7,500 per night for two bedrooms or $8,140 for four bedrooms, but you'll be told—if you ask—that these suites "generally are not rented." They're usually reserved for visiting royalty or high-rolling gamblers.

MOVING ON ...

Ready to move on? The Mirage is just next door, sharing a hundred-acre site with Treasure Island, its younger companion. In these two resorts (both owned by Mirage Resorts, Inc.), you'll find enough child-pleasing entertainment to keep the family occupied for at least a week. If you're approaching them from inside Caesars Palace, allow some extra time for wandering around the huge complex while hunting for the nearest exit. Muscular centurions, helmeted and armored, will help you find your way.

Once outside Caesars on your way to the south entrance of the Mirage, you may notice the **Brahma Shrine**. It is a small, colorful Thai-Buddhist shrine, often decked with fresh flowers from grateful visitors, who say their wishes have been granted after meditation there. Some call it "the good luck shrine." Copied from an original Brahma shrine in Bangkok, Thailand, this one was a joint gift to Caesars from a Thai newspaper tycoon and a Hong Kong businessman.

Just beyond the arch that leads to The Forum Shops, you can step aboard another moving sidewalk to carry you into the Mirage. Or, for the full effect of entering a timeless Polynesian paradise, you can keep walking north to the Mirage main entrance.

THE MIRAGE—
A POLYNESIAN PARADISE

In daylight you're attracted by waterfalls and grottos and jungle greenery in the middle of a lagoon that separates the resort from the street. At night you join crowds on the sidewalk to watch the volcano, a man-made mountain fifty-four feet tall, as it erupts in a shower of fireworks every fifteen minutes from dusk to midnight.

As soon as you step inside, you hear the soothing splash of more water. Stroll through groves of real banana palms and tropical vines in a nine-story rainforest atrium, where an invisible computerized misting system keeps the air just humid enough to make you feel like you're in Hawaii. Even the orchids are real.

The Mirage
3400 Las Vegas Boulevard South
Las Vegas, NV 89109
General information: (702) 791-7111
Room reservations: (800) 627-6667
Inside Nevada: (702) 731-7222
Fax: (702) 791-7414
Rates: from $79, Sunday–Thursday;
$99, Friday & Saturday

In the carpeted lobby, a fifty-three-foot glass wall behind the registration desk reveals a coral reef aquarium, where more than a thousand sharks, rays, and angelfish swim in twenty thousand gallons of saltwater. Visitors—especially children—seem endlessly fascinated by these reef creatures from seas around the world. The fish have been gathered from the oceans around Australia, Fiji, Tonga, and Hawaii and from the Sea of Cortez, the Red Sea, and the Caribbean. Even more fascinating are two animal habitats for the bottle-nosed dolphins and white Bengal tigers who live at the Mirage.

White Bengal Tigers—In Nevada?

If you came in through the south entrance, you saw the tigers as soon as you stepped off the moving walkway. During shows in Theatre Mirage, some tigers may be on stage with Siegfried and Roy, the illusionists who brought them here, but they spend off-duty time in their climate-controlled habitat . . . when they're not outdoors at Jungle Palace, Siegfried and Roy's home near Las Vegas. At different times you may see different tigers—they rotate their city appearances—but you can see tigers in the habitat at any time of day, seven days a week.

Behind slanted glass windows (designed to protect the tigers from the glare of casino lights and camera flashes), the big cats climb and jump on rock ledges, snooze in a cave, or lounge beside their own swimming pool. Sometimes they plunge into the water for a swim. Video screens above the viewing windows show continuous recorded commentary by Siegfried and Roy, with scenes of tigers in their outdoor home.

In the **Theatre Mirage** (around the corner from the habitat and to the left), **Siegfried and Roy** perform with the tigers three weeks a month, with a week off between runs while other performers take over the stage. Their magic show is often sold out, so it's smart to book seats in advance. Usual showtimes are twice nightly, 7:30 and 11 P.M., except Wednesdays. For show schedules, ticket prices, and reservations, phone the ticket office at (702) 792-7777.

Where Will We Find the Dolphins?

Signs with arrows direct you through the casino and past the Street of Shops to the outdoor dolphin habitat, where seven bottle-nosed dolphins attract daily crowds. Thousands of schoolchildren come to the habitat with their teachers every year to learn about dolphins in an environmental education program developed by the Clark County School System and the Mirage dolphin project.

When you visit the friendly sea creatures, you'll join one of several small groups led by trained naturalists, who tell you about the animals, their origins, and their habits. You'll watch the dolphins swim and leap in their million-gallon pool, then you'll move underground for an aquarium-style underwater view. Occasionally, a curious dolphin swims toward the window for a closer view of human spectators.

The Mirage dolphin policy, you are told, is to take no dolphins from the wild. The five original adult dolphins were already in captivity before being brought to Las Vegas from aquarium habitats. Two others were born at the Mirage. You may be shown a video of the birth of one of these babies. They're also subjects of countless crayon drawings by children whose work is exhibited in the Habitat Shop.

   The Dolphin Habitat is open from 11 A.M. to 7 P.M., Monday through Friday, and 9 A.M. to 7 P.M. on Saturday and Sunday.

If You're Staying at the Mirage . . .

You and your family will find a bright Polynesian theme in your own haven among the 3,054 rooms and suites. Posted rates are high, from $79 to $350 a night, starting at $99 on weekends, but you can ask your travel agent about special package rates that include airfare. Suites are available at $450 for one bedroom, $600 to $800 for two bedrooms. There's no charge for children twelve and younger, but the 8 percent room tax is added daily. Six lanai bungalows, each with a private pool and garden, and eight villa apartments aren't listed on the rate card.

Food and Refreshments at the Mirage

Whether or not you're a hotel guest, the Mirage makes you and your family feel welcome in the restaurants and shops. On a hot summer day, the atrium is a cool oasis. When you sit down in the **Lagoon Saloon** and order a Mai-Tai or Singapore Sling, the kids can have soft drinks or juice. Frazzled parents begin to feel relaxed as sunlight filters through the palm leaves, and waterfalls make soothing music. **Coconuts Ice Cream Shop** is another favorite stop for weary sight-seers on their way to or from the dolphin habitat—just the spot for an impromptu ice-cream cone or frozen yogurt. From the **Dolphin Snack Bar**, you can watch the dolphins at play. On the other side of the swimming pool, the **Paradise Cafe** offers a view of human swimmers, in season. Closer to the tigers, the **California Pizza Kitchen** is handy for a casual lunch or dinner.

The **Mirage Buffet** is a family favorite—one of the best buffets in town with lots of space, cheerful decor, excellent food, and more than sixty menu items every day. Breakfast is served from 7 to 10:45 A.M., lunch from 11 A.M. to 2:45 P.M., and dinner from 3 to 9:30 P.M. On Sundays, champagne brunch and dinner attracts crowds from 8 A.M. to 9:30 P.M.

Any time you want table service, the **Caribe Cafe** is open around-the-clock for breakfast, lunch, and dinner. And when you're ready for a leisurely, elegant meal, the Mirage has five specialty restaurants.

Fine Dining at the Mirage

Kokomo's, with an open-air feeling and a view of jungle waterfalls, specializes in fresh seafood and aged steaks at lunch and dinner. Breakfast is served on certain days, but it's best to check the schedule.

Mikado is the teppan-style Japanese restaurant, where agile cooks perform like jugglers as they conjure up your dinner. There's also a sushi bar. Next door at **Moongate**, you'll find classic Cantonese and Szechuan dishes elegantly served in a tranquil Chinese courtyard setting.

The Bistro takes you to Paris for traditional French cuisine amid paintings of Lautrec and Degas. Around the corner and down a cobblestone street, **Ristorante Riva** serves regional Italian dishes—homemade pastas, fresh seafood, and a variety of veal recipes. (Be sure to check out the lifelike Italian housewife near the entrance, carrying her shopping bag into a domestic doorway.)

With the exception of **Kokomo's**, all these specialty restaurants serve dinner only. Reservations are suggested; call (702) 791-7111 to book a table.

TREASURE ISLAND—
FOR BUCCANEER HOSPITALITY

When you're ready to move on to Treasure Island, the other half of Stephen Wynn's fantasy creation on the Strip, it doesn't take long to travel from the timeless rain forest to an eighteenth-century pirate village. Step outside the Mirage main entrance and turn left. Those people waiting in line beside the trolley tracks know where they're going. Every four minutes or so, a brass-trimmed shuttle-trolley glides to a stop outside the Mirage. Climb aboard and you're on your way to a pirate adventure reminiscent of *Treasure Island,* Robert Louis Stevenson's classic adventure story, complete with buried treasure and a live sea battle.

Treasure Island
3300 Las Vegas Boulevard South
Las Vegas, NV 89109
General information: (702) 894-7111
Room reservations: (800) 944-7444
Fax: (702) 894-7414
Rates: from $59, Sunday–Thursday;
$129, Friday & Saturday

Arriving by tram, you enter Treasure Island near the parking garage, at the top of an escalator leading down to the shopping promenade. But if you arrive by car or taxi and are staying at the resort, you'll be greeted at the main entrance by genial pirates in ruffled shirts, knee breeches, and three-cornered hats. A pirate will take charge of your luggage while you and your family head for the registration counter. Other visitors may be waiting ahead of you as busy desk clerks consult computer screens, but you won't have to wait long unless you've arrived during a rush of group tours or conventions.

There's a Caribbean feeling in the lobby—polished tile floors, dark woodwork, sunlight filtering through beveled-glass doors trimmed with gleaming brass—but you know it's Las Vegas when you hear the clatter of slot machines in the casino. On your way to the elevators, you'll notice several restaurants and a corridor of shops you'll want to explore after claiming your room.

Open the door to a spacious, cheerful room with at least one floor-to-ceiling window serving up a view of the city, desert hills, and lots of sky.

If your room faces the Strip, you can look down on Buccaneer Bay, site of the sea battle your children are clamoring to see. Watch the battle from your room, then see it again from the sidewalk. If your room overlooks the swimming pool with its water slides and palm trees, you'll also have a nighttime view of the erupting volcano in front of the Mirage. Windows are sealed for safety, but there's a narrow strip in the middle you can open to admit fresh air.

This is one of 2,900 Treasure Island guest rooms, including 212 suites, in three 36-story towers. Room rates change often (usually up, but sometimes down). A recent range started at $59 during the week and $129 on weekends, but the only way to be sure is to phone the resort for information. Ask your travel agent about package plans that include airfare. Mirage rates are always higher, but the two companion resorts have some mutual arrangements. When you dine in Mirage restaurants, for example, you can charge those meals to your room at Treasure Island—and it works both ways.

Once you've settled in, it's time to explore the rest of Treasure Island. If the time is late afternoon, there'll be no argument about where to go first. The main attraction is on Buccaneer Bay, every ninety minutes from 4:30 P.M. until midnight, in good weather. Showtimes are posted near the dock.

Pirates Are the Good Guys

You don't need a ticket to see this show. Buccaneer Bay is right on the Strip, where the sidewalk becomes a wooden dock leading to Treasure Island. Everyone can enjoy this convincingly realistic sea battle between a British frigate and an eighteenth-century pirate ship. You can also watch it from a dockside cantina overlooking the bay and from some hotel rooms, but the best view of all is from the sidewalk. The crowd starts forming at least thirty minutes before showtime, so be prepared to stand around for a while if you want a front-row view of the action.

While you wait, you can listen to the sound of seagulls and watch pirates unloading barrels of booty from the deck of a sailing ship, the *Hispañola*. Their hideaway is tucked behind a rugged cliff with a skull and crossbones etched into its face. On shore, the village seems busy, with moving figures visible behind lighted windows and wrought-iron balconies.

Suddenly, HMS *Britannia* sails around the point, and a British captain challenges the pirates to surrender.

When the brigands refuse, the action begins. Both ships fire their cannons as men scramble across decks, swing from ropes, tumble from tall masts, and leap into the water. Flames shoot into the air as cannons thunder. Before the battle is over, one ship has sunk and the other seems demolished, with broken masts and a ruined hull.

The illusion is so convincing that some small children may find it frightening. It's a noisy battle, and the flames are so real you can actually feel the heat from where you stand on the dock. But most children, while holding a parent's hand or from a safe perch on a father's shoulders, seem to recognize that this is "just pretend." They're reassured after the show when they watch the "sunken" ships rise to the surface. Within an hour, broken masts are miraculously repaired, and actors are back on deck, ready to wage another battle.

Incidentally, there's a delightful one-hour movie for children shown on Treasure Island's in-house television channel. Filmed especially for the resort, it tells the story of a young boy who visits Treasure Island with his parents and finds himself involved with real pirates in a search for buried treasure. I won't give away the plot . . . except to tell you that the baby-sitter looks a lot like Long John Silver. See it in your room almost anytime. It's repeated at regular intervals, day and night.

International Magic: Cirque de Soleil

Treasure Island has it's own fifteen-hundred-seat show-room specifically built to exhibit *Mystere,* a lavishly costumed spectacle staged by **Cirque de Soleil**, a French Canadian circus company from Montreal. Intriguing snippets from the show are projected, nonstop,

on a video screen above the escalator leading from Treasure Island's self-parking garage down to the
theater and shopping promenade. These scenes, accompanied by rhythmic drums, are the first things you see
when you enter Treasure Island from the garage. Smaller
versions of the same scenes appear on television screens
aboard the shuttle-trolley connecting Treasure Island
with the Mirage.

Other Treasure Island Attractions

At the end of the shopping promenade, just beyond
the escalator, a stone gate suggests the entrance to a Moor-
ish castle. This is **Mutiny Bay**, an entertainment center
designed especially for visitors too young for the casino
area. In alcoves beside the gate, two animated skeletons of
former residents greet visitors and exchange comments.

Inside you find video games, motion simulators, pin-
ball, and carnival-style skill-testers offering toy prizes.
From the central stone courtyard, you can explore the
Enchanted Chamber to find games designed for
younger children, **The Armory** for video games, or the
Map Room to study a treasure map. Background
sounds of seaport bustle and pirate voices contribute to
the illusion of a mutineers' hideaway. At intervals, a robotic resident of Mutiny Bay leans out her window and
shouts in Spanish to an unseen pirate in the crowd.

Don't Forget Breakfast, Lunch, and Dinner, Matey

Meals in Treasure Island's restaurants range from
casual snacks to elegant feasts. Choose a spot to suit
your family and the time of day.

The **Lookout Cafe**, open twenty-four hours a day, is a favorite with children because it overlooks the swimming pool. (Prepare to be reminded that you simply *must* reserve time to test those water slides.) The children's menu, in the shape of a pirate hat, is another kid-pleaser. So are breakfasts, from granola to pancakes and sausage. Lunch and dinner menus list moderate prices.

Treasure Island Buffets offer three different settings with menus to match: Chinese, Italian, and American. The **Black Spot Grille**, open for dinner only, is a sidewalk cafe without the sidewalk. Freshly prepared pastas and salads are served in a casual atmosphere, and prices are reasonable. **The Plank** is the place to splurge on mesquite-grilled steaks, chops, or lobster in a warm, candle-lit library lined with bookcases. The old books are real.

The **Seven Seas Snack Bar** serves breakfast, then focuses on seafood chowders, sandwiches, and burgers. **Smuggler's Cantina**, in the shopping promenade, is open for lunch and dinner on the run. Carry your own tray and order a Mexican dish or sandwich and coffee. **Sweet Revenge** tempts ice-cream sundae fans to ignore the slimming diet, but calorie-counters can order frozen yogurt.

At the **Buccaneer Bay Club**, reached by private elevator, you can watch the battle (provided you get a window table) as pirates confront British sailors in the bay below. The menu is varied and nothing is cheap.

For a Quick Purchase . . .

No matter how efficient you were when you packed for this trip, it's almost inevitable that you'll need to buy something. Besides, it's fun to browse in these shops.

Loot n' Booty is the place for newspapers and magazines, film, toothpaste, and other sundries. The **Buccaneer Bay Shoppe** and **The Crow's Nest** provide souvenirs with the Treasure Island logo and magic stuff recalling Cirque de Soleil.

Captain Kid's lures youngsters with displays of plush animals and toys. **The Treasure Chest** appeals to luxury lovers who like expensive jewelry and watches. And **Damsels in Dis'Dress** (if you can forgive the awful pun) is a boutique well stocked with women's clothing and accessories. Some prices are surprisingly reasonable.

When your Treasure Island visit is over, don't be surprised if your kids don't want to leave. Just remind them that there's a lot more to see in Las Vegas, and time is running out . . .

CHAPTER 5

Still on the Strip

By this time, you know why you're not going to see all of Las Vegas in one visit. Just as you can't eat everything on one of those sumptuous casino buffets in one meal, you can't absorb the many facets of this city in a day or two. You can choose to concentrate on a few attractions or skim the surface of many. If you start with the Strip, be sure to save time for other parts of Las Vegas and some of the surrounding desert.

So far we've concentrated on the newest big resorts at the south end of Las Vegas Boulevard; there's a lot more to see on the Strip alone. You'll discover surprises in every block. Heading north, in the two-mile stretch between Spring Mountain Road and Sahara Avenue, you'll pass some of the huge casinos that made headlines in the 1950s and '60s: the **Desert Inn**, the **Stardust**, the **Riviera**, and the **Sahara**. Many of the streets you cross are named for these resorts.

In the same neighborhood, you'll find newer attractions, such as Grand Slam Canyon at Circus Circus and the Wet 'n' Wild water park. Your itinerary will be determined by the number and ages of your children, their personal preferences, and your own stamina. If they've been asking, "What's under that big pink bubble?" your next destination has to be Grand Slam Canyon, a five-acre indoor amusement park designed for children and adults.

CIRCUS CIRCUS REVISITED

Long before other Las Vegas casinos began making special provisions for children, **Circus Circus** entertained families with a carnival midway and circus acts under a big permanent tent. When it opened in 1968, the modest casino had no hotel rooms, but parents could bring their children to see an elephant, to eat popcorn and cotton candy, and come away with toy prizes from carnival games.

How the Circus has grown! The casino's first four hundred hotel rooms were added in 1972, offering bargain accommodations. Now the expanded hotel complex has twenty-eight hundred rooms in towers dominating a sixty-nine-acre site on the Las Vegas Strip. Each room has two queen-sized beds or one king-size, but rates are still budget-priced, among the lowest in Las Vegas. Smokers are separated from nonsmokers on different floors.

Travelers with motor homes and camper vehicles may drive into the adjacent **Circusland RV Park** and hook up utilities in one of 358 landscaped spaces. The park has its own swimming pool, saunas, jacuzzis, fenced pet runs, and a kiddie playground. There's also a twenty-four-hour convenience store, a Laundromat, and a game arcade. And the big casino is just a few steps away.

Inside the central hotel-casino building, an updated circus arena occupies the mezzanine. Every day, 11 A.M. to midnight, you can watch acrobats, jugglers, trapeze artists, and clowns in live performances. Circus Circus ads remind you that this is "the only showroom in Nevada where the entertainment is FREE . . . with no need for tickets or reservations." On the fringes of the arena, electronic arcade games have joined traditional carnival booths to attract the multitudes. Much of this was going on before August 1993, when Circus Circus Enterprises opened its $90 million theme park.

Grand Slam Canyon

Under an enormous pink "adventuredome," there's a climate-controlled amusement park designed to reflect the evolution of southwestern canyon country, from the age of dinosaurs to the present.

Grand Slam Canyon *at Circus Circus*
2880 Las Vegas Boulevard South
Open daily, 10 A.M. to 10 P.M. (subject to change). Call for current prices and schedules: (702) 734-0410

Indoor winding paths lead you through narrow passes and tunnels, past sandstone cliffs, grottos, and caves. **Grand Slam Falls** cascades sixty-eight feet from the top of an indoor mountain.

Canyon Blaster is the centerpiece, a roller coaster with dizzying double-loops and steep drops, turning riders upside down from time to time while zooming around the pink-lighted interior. It's a thrill ride not recommended for very young children. A child must be at least 48 inches tall, and there's a measuring gauge at the entrance. At the end of the ride, you may see a photo of yourself, snapped in midscream.

Canyon Cars allow wild drivers to bump into each other for fun, but the driver must measure up to the 54-inch mark (and nobody shorter than 48 inches is allowed to ride). **Rim Runner** is a water-chute ride, forerunner of Grand Canyon Rapids at MGM. Expect to get a bit wet as your raft races down mountain rapids and through a tunnel to the final splashdown. This one's less restricted, but rafters have to be 42 inches or taller. Same height is required for **Sand Pirates**, a swinging pirate ship that swoops above the canyon, suspending you for a heart-stopping moment at the high point.

Small children aren't neglected. Their own special rides include child-sized airplanes called **Thunderbirds**, and a gentle Ferris wheel, **Drifters**, whose seats are designed to look like small hot-air balloons. **Miner Mike** is a mini–roller coaster, off-limits to big people taller than 54 inches (but riders have to measure at least 33 inches). **Road Runner** and **B.C. Plus** are billed as rides for the whole family yet are tame enough for toddlers. At the **Fossil Dig**, children dig in the sand surrounded by replicas of ancient fossils imbedded in the artificial rock. Next door at **Cliffhangers**, adventurous youngsters test their skill at net-climbing and ball-crawl games as they scramble through slides and tunnels.

Along the **Passage of Time**, murals depicting the evolution of dinosaurs are a backdrop for a compact habitat that looks like a corner of Jurassic Park. Lifelike automated dinosaurs are favorites with some very small naturalists.

At the opposite end of the pink dome, older children and adults can file in to a black-lit arena for a game of **Hot Shots Laser Tag**, a high-tech interactive game played with laser guns. Lots of action in an unreal world. Not far away, there's a video arcade and a carnival midway. Some families discover the **Mystic Magic Theater** and stop to watch illusionists on stage. Others browse at the **Trading Post** or consult their Grand Slam maps to choose a place for lunch or a snack.

La Cantina, up a stairway near the Mystic Magic Theater, serves up spicy southwestern dishes, margaritas for adults, and the illusion of a cliffside retreat overlooking the canyon. **Bronto Brew and Cookies** is within easy reach of the kiddie rides, and the **Outpost Cafe**, near Cliffhangers, is a handy place for hot dogs, nachos, and other quick snacks. Food and beverage carts are scattered around the park for instant satisfaction.

A general-admission ticket allows you to spend the day at Grand Slam Canyon with a free ride included. Or you can buy an all-day pass with unlimited rides and go in and out as many times as you like. When you phone for current prices and schedules, ask about special rates for young children, military personnel, and seniors.

If you're ready to leave Grand Slam Canyon for a meal, you'll find more restaurants inside the casino.

Circus Circus Restaurants

The **Pink Pony Coffee Shop** and the **Skyrise Dining Room** are open twenty-four hours a day. Each has a special menu for children as well as a full selection for adults. **The Circus Buffet** offers breakfast, lunch, and dinner at bargain prices, and the **Steak House** is the casino's top candlelight-and-wine restaurant for dinner. There's a **McDonald's** on the mezzanine midway, and the **Circus Pizzeria** is on the main level.

Eventually, you'll have to tear yourself away from the fun at Circus Circus. There's still more to do on Las Vegas Boulevard.

WATER FUN ON THE STRIP

No need to abandon water play in this desert city. Water babies and their parents, those who usually head for beaches in summer, will find swimming pools at most hotels and motels. Lavish pool complexes at the big resorts are spectacular. If you visit the Tropicana, for example, you'll see an indoor-outdoor pool covering 13,500 square feet.

And then there's **Wet 'n Wild**, a whole theme park dedicated to the delights of water. It's right on the Strip, across the boulevard from Circus Circus.

Wet 'n Wild
Las Vegas Boulevard, just south
of Sahara Avenue
Open daily, April–October
Hours: Usually 10 A.M. to 6 P.M.
(subject to change)
Call for admission prices: (702) 734-0088;
ask about discounts and two-day tickets

More than a million gallons of water flow thorough this enormous water park. River, lake, or ocean? Name your preference. White-water rapids, gentle streams, waterfalls, and slides keep you pleasantly soaked and moving from one attraction to another. There's even a wave pool—a half million gallons of undulating water . . . without sharks.

At the **Children's Playground**, even the tiniest paddlers will be entertained. They can sail aboard small unsinkable boats in a shallow lake or wade in a sheltered pool. On the **Lazy River**, the whole family can simply float along on an inflated raft.

Thrill-seekers may relish the spiraling **Hydra Maniac** and the free fall at **Bomb Bay**. They'll also want to explore the mystery of the **Black Hole** and tumble along on the **Raging Rapids**. Big swimmers can test their surfboard skills on a mechanical board. And for exhausted sight-seers, there's a broad expanse of green turf near the **Wave Pool** with lounge chairs for relaxing in sunshine or shade.

Parking is free, or you can get there by Las Vegas Strip Trolley or CAT (Citizens Area Transit) bus, Route #302. After entering the park, you'll be directed to dressing rooms, where you can change into swimsuits. Lockers and towels are provided. But watch out for that desert sun! Be liberal with the sunscreen. When the temperature is 110° F, you're safer in the shade.

OTHER ATTRACTIONS ON THE STRIP

On the other side of Las Vegas Boulevard, a half block north of Circus Circus, you'll find a little museum that's a popular stop on tour bus itineraries.

Guinness World of Records Museum
2780 Las Vegas Boulevard South
Open daily, including holidays
Hours: 9 A.M. to 9 P.M. Call for admission
prices: (702) 792-0640

Improve your trivia score with facts about the biggest, tiniest, fastest, oldest, record-breaking curiosities listed in the *Guinness Book of Records*. Life-sized replicas, exhibits, computerized data banks, interactive displays, and color videos bring them to life.

Moving On ...

Head back toward Circus Circus and keep going south until you reach the Stardust. Directly across the street, facing the Desert Inn, you'll find an indoor playground for the computer age. This one's not for very small children, but teens and adults won't be intimidated—not if they're familiar with the simulated violence of arcade video games.

Virtual World
3055 Las Vegas Boulevard South
Open Sunday–Thursday, 11 A.M. to 11 P.M.
Friday & Saturday, 11 A.M. to 3 A.M. Call
for prices and schedules: (702) 369-3583

Sophisticated video games with special effects take you inside virtual worlds, where you become a participant. You're not just standing there maneuvering a handle; instead, you sit in a cockpit, put on a pair of magic goggles, and become a space pilot or tank gunner, ready to compete with game players in other virtual worlds— maybe Dallas, San Diego, Chicago, or Tokyo.

Space buffs can join a game of Red Planet and speed across the rocky surface of Mars in a hovercraft. You're at the controls, but look out for those other space vehicles racing toward you!

Macho gamesters may prefer BattleTech, a chance to shoot everything in sight without really hurting anybody. The object is to blast your opponents before they blast you. From the top of a "walking" tank in a desert battle-ground, aim your laser gun and fire. If you blow up more tanks than the other players, you win. Definitely *not* a tame game!

When you call Virtual World for prices and schedules, you won't reach an actual human being, but a virtual voice will welcome you to "the world's first digital theme park" and will tell you which buttons to push.

Moving On . . .

Around the corner and a block east of the Strip, on the way to the Las Vegas Convention Center, there's a new entertainment museum which opened in 1994.

Debbie Reynolds Hollywood Motion Picture Museum
in the Debbie Reynolds Hotel
305 Convention Center Drive
Open daily, 9 A.M. to 10 P.M.
(702) 734-0711

Now that the longtime movie actress and showroom performer has a hotel with her name on it, she also has a place to exhibit her huge private collection of Hollywood memorabilia. Multimedia displays (using vintage film clips, costumes, and props) trace the history of movies from silent days to the present. **Monday Night at the Movies** offers full-length features. Call to find out what's playing.

Moving On . . .

Back on the Strip, head south and cross Sands Avenue. (It becomes Spring Mountain Road on the opposite side of Las Vegas Boulevard.) Keep going, past Treasure Island and the Mirage on your right, past Casino Royale and Harrah's on your left. At the Imperial Palace Hotel, you'll find another special museum.

Imperial Palace Auto Collection
in the Imperial Palace Hotel
parking garage
3535 Las Vegas Boulevard
Open daily, 9:30 A.M. to 11:30 P.M.
Call for admission prices:
(702) 794-3174

Famous and infamous automobiles, including Adolf Hitler's 1939 Mercedes sedan, are displayed in a comfortable fifth-floor gallery. Appropriately enough, the gallery is built into the hotel's parking garage, but the plush decor of the Duesenberg Room, Presidents' Row, Leaders' Row, and Legends Lane is a far cry from self-parking.

The collection includes more than eight hundred vehicles, but you won't see all of them at once. Changing exhibits feature about two hundred at a time. There's always a mixture of antique and classic cars, along with trucks, motorcycles, and "special interest" vehicles once used by celebrities.

The Imperial Palace also offers a weekly poolside **Waikiki-style luau** with hula dancers and music along with a tropical feast. Ask about it when you phone.

Moving On . . .

While you're in the neighborhood, there's one more show-biz museum worth a visit. In the shadow of the Flamingo Hilton, look for the glittering marquee that resembles one on a movie theater.

Retonio's Magic and Movie Hall of Fame
at O'Sheas Hilton Casino
3555 Las Vegas Boulevard South
Open daily, 10 A.M. to midnight
Call for current prices and schedules:
(702) 792-0788

Kids, parents, and fans of mystifying illusions can spend an hour or so watching live magic shows and browsing through exhibits of old-time arcade machines. Ventriloquists, escape artists, and illusionists give demonstrations every hour in the **Houdini Theater**. Twice nightly there's a full-length stage production in the same theater.

Moving On . . .

There's still so much to see and do—so many choices to make. It's hard to pull yourself away from the Strip and its nonstop attractions. If your children are old enough to stay up late once in a while, you may decide to see one of the lavish stage productions Las Vegas is famous for. Some showrooms now schedule special early shows with families in mind.

WHERE THE STARS ARE

We've already mentioned some shows of special interest to children at Excalibur, Luxor, Caesars Palace, Treasure Island, and the Mirage. Other casino showrooms offer family-oriented productions from time to time. At the **Las Vegas Hilton**, Andrew Lloyd Webber's *Starlight Express* (a musical about trains, with dancers on roller skates) has been a long-running favorite. **Harrah's** has staged *Spellbound: A Concert of Illusion,* and several other casinos often include country-western stars in their roster of entertainers. Programs do change, so you'll need current information about headliners, schedules, and prices.

Weekend editions of the *Las Vegas Sun* include a magazine, *Showbiz Weekly,* that features articles and ads about current entertainment, along with a directory of showrooms and restaurants. Another good source is *What's On in Las Vegas,* a free magazine distributed through most hotels. If you don't find a copy in your room, ask the concierge or bell captain for a list of current shows with telephone numbers to call to reserve tickets. Some ticket prices include tip and taxes. If you're not sure, ask.

Here's a list of the major showrooms. Some shows are suitable for children, others aren't. Again, it's easy to find out—just ask.

Aladdin Hotel The Showroom (702) 736-0111

Bally's Las Vegas Celebrity Room (702) 739-4111

Caesars Palace Circus Maximus (702) 631-7110

Debbie Reynolds Hotel Star Theater (702) 734-0711

Excalibur King Arthur's Arena (702) 597-7600

Flamingo Hilton Showroom (702) 733-3111

Hacienda Hotel Fiesta Showroom (702) 739-8911

Harrah's Las Vegas Commander's Theatre
          (702) 369-5000

Imperial Palace Imperial Theatre (702) 794-3261

Las Vegas Hilton Showroom (702) 732-5755

Luxor Pharaoh's Dinner Theatre (702) 262-4900

MGM Grand Hotel Grand Theatre (702) 891-7777
          Hollywood Theatre (800) 929-1111

The Mirage Theatre Mirage (702) 791-7111

Rio Suite Hotel Copa Cabana Showroom
          (702) 252-7777

Riviera Hotel Versailles Theatre (702) 794-9433

Sahara Hotel Congo Theatre (702) 737-2515

Sheraton Desert Inn Crystal Room (702) 733-4566

Stardust Hotel Stardust Theatre (702) 732-6213

Treasure Island Cirque du Soleil (702) 894-7111

Tropicana Resort Tiffany Showroom (702) 739-2411

Vegas World Galaxy Theatre (702) 383-5264

Westward Ho The Crown Room (702) 731-2900

CHAPTER 6

The Other Las Vegas

Once you're ready to venture beyond the Strip, the rest of Las Vegas is waiting to be explored. There are neighborhoods where children ride bikes and play hopscotch and toss balls, just as they would in any other city. They meet after school in playgrounds and parks, they attend churches, synagogues, or mosques, and they join their parents in excursions to local museums and outdoor attractions. Nearly a million people live in Las Vegas.

You may choose to head out in any direction, but "downtown" is just up the street and worth a visit. After decades of decline in the shadow of the glamorous Strip, downtown Las Vegas is getting a face-lift—a new look designed to appeal to families.

Take a look at a good map of the city. North of Sahara Avenue, you're inside the Las Vegas city limits. Keep going up Las Vegas Boulevard and cross Charleston Boulevard. Now you're officially downtown, the birthplace of modern Las Vegas. This is an older part of the city, where streets are laid out in neat rectangles and are much closer together than streets crossing the Strip. This is where you'll find City Hall, the county courthouse, old banks, and office buildings. It looks very much like down-town areas in many small western cities . . . until you come to **Fremont Street** and the neighborhood affec-tionately called **Glitter Gulch**.

Old-time Las Vegans are sentimental about down-town. It has been part of their history since the city was incorporated in 1905. Fremont Street was the first to be paved in 1925 and the first to have a traffic light. The city's first gaming license was issued to a downtown casino in the 1930s, and Fremont Street became a gambler's mecca with a Wild West image. The city's first elevator was in the Apache Hotel, and the first high-rise hotel was the Fremont, opened in 1956.

When big, shiny, new casino-resorts on the Strip started attracting much bigger crowds in the '40s and '50s, downtown hotels lost business but kept their raff-ish reputation. Today, Fremont Street still sparkles at night with colored lights and neon signs as it has for decades, beckoning gamblers to casinos such as Binion's Horseshoe, Lady Luck, the Four Queens, Fitzgerald's, and Sam Boyd's Fremont.

Traditionally, the neighborhood has not been a place to take children. During the years when such entertainers as Elvis Presley, Frank Sinatra, and Sammy Davis Jr. were attracting dressed-up couples to big showrooms on the Strip, dwindling downtown crowds were mostly men who were there to gamble—and they left their families at home.

In recent years, the downtown atmosphere has grown slightly more sedate, especially since Stephen Wynn bought the Golden Nugget Casino, built a hotel on the site, and turned it into a plush resort. Other Glitter Gulch casinos upgraded their images, too, but there seemed to be no way for crowded Fremont Street to compete with the spacious palaces on the Strip. Downtown was increasingly ignored by tourists.

A visitor profile study, conducted monthly and reported annually for the Las Vegas Convention & Visitors Authority, recently found that seven in ten visitors said they had visited downtown during their stay. Most of the others, when asked why they didn't go downtown, said they didn't have enough time, or they preferred the Strip, or they simply weren't interested in downtown. Now the city's redevelopment agency is trying to change that feeling. Once the face-lift is complete, Fremont Street will be more family-friendly.

EXPLORING DOWNTOWN

Beyond the glitz of Fremont Street, the history of Nevada pioneers is preserved in museums and in a few old buildings that have survived the city's growth. If you start at the Union Plaza Hotel, 1 Main Street, you're standing at the edge of the original Las Vegas Townsite laid out in 1905.

Strolling around the old streets, it's possible to imagine what Las Vegas was like some ninety years ago, when it was just a small railroad town. To appreciate the accidents of history that led to the growth of a town in this specific spot, look back several centuries.

In ancient times, Native American tribes knew they could find freshwater springs in this uninhabited valley, so they stopped here from time to time in their travels through the desert. In the 1770s, when the area was part of New Mexico, Spanish surveyors discovered the oasis and called it Las Vegas, "The Meadows." Later, American explorer and mapmaker John C. Fremont stopped at the Las Vegas springs and published an 1844 description that led more and more California-bound travelers to pause for water at the Big Springs. Paiute Indians were still in the valley (as they are today), but most early white travelers ignored any prior rights the Native Americans might have had.

In 1855, eleven years after Fremont's report, Mormon colonists from Utah built a fortified mission just a few blocks north of the Union Plaza Hotel (see Old Las Vegas Mormon Fort, later in this chapter). The missionary-colonists intended to convert the Indians, but they gave up after two years and sold the land to a rancher, Octavius D. Gass.

The property remained a working ranch, after Archibald Stewart took it over, until 1902. That year Stewart's widow sold the land to Senator William J. Clark of Montana for his San Pedro–Los Angeles–Salt Lake Railroad. Once the new rail line was finished in 1905, Clark auctioned off some of the railroad's land as separate lots in his "Las Vegas Townsite." Those lots became the heart of downtown, a neat grid of numbered and named streets close to the railroad.

The original town was only five blocks wide: from Main Street, along the railroad, to Fifth Street—now Las Vegas Boulevard. North to south, it extended eight blocks from Stewart Avenue to Garces. Walking around in that area today, you find a few landmarks still standing in the shadow of casinos. Some have been there since the '20s and '30s. The oldest have survived even longer, since the early railroad maintenance buildings, some built in 1908, and the first company bungalows were constructed for railroad workers and their families. Here's where you'll find the historic structures and sites—most of them very close to Fremont Street.

Historic Structures and Sites

The Union Plaza Hotel

Located at 1 Main Street at Fremont, this is not the original building on this site, but it covers the spot where the first Las Vegas depot stood in the early days, dominating the downtown streetscape. Waiting passengers once mingled with town residents in a tree-shaded park in front of the old mission-style depot. That building was replaced in 1940, but the ghosts of early travelers may still hover around the modern hotel with its neon facade. Where else would you find a hotel with a train station in the lobby? If you travel to Las Vegas by Amtrak, this is where you'll step off the train.

The Victory Hotel

Situated at 307 North Main, the Victory is the oldest remaining downtown hotel. Opened in 1910 as the Lincoln Hotel, a haven for rail travelers, it was close to the old depot and echoed its mission-style architecture.

The Ice Plant

One of two surviving buildings from the original railroad complex, located at 612 South Main, the Ice Plant was built in 1908 by a railroad subsidiary, the Pacific Fruit and Express Company. It manufactured ice for seventy-five years, until 1983.

Railroad Storehouse Building

Located at 700 Dividend Drive, this is out of the way for a stroll, but you can see it from the Union Plaza, on the other side of the tracks. Constructed in 1910 as Hanson Hall, it doubled as a storehouse for equipment and a social center for railroad workers.

Railroad Cottages
Built by the railroad for its workers, these company-town homes once filled four blocks, from Garces to Clark between Second Street (now Casino Center Boulevard) and Fourth Street. Originally, there were sixty-four concrete-block bungalows, each with four or five rooms. A few still stand, including eight in a row in the 600 block of Third Street.

El Portal Theater
The city's first modern movie theater, at 310 East Fremont, the El Portal opened in 1928. Owners Ernie Cragin and William Pike spent $150,000 to make it a luxurious picture palace. Did these early entrepreneurs dream about multi-million-dollar showrooms in a future Las Vegas?

The Apache Hotel
In the shadow of Binion's Horseshoe Casino, at 128 Fremont Street, the Apache has survived more than three decades of change in downtown Las Vegas. When it opened in 1931, it was considered the city's most elegant hotel. Sight-seers often strolled through the lobby and timidly tested the elevator, the first in town. Soon after World War II, the Apache was sold to Benny Binion, a Texan with a shady past, who also bought the Eldorado Casino next door and expanded the two into a single operation. Look inside Binion's Horseshoe to see a hundred U.S. banknotes, worth $10,000 each in the 1870s, preserved between sheets of bullet-proof glass and suspended from a giant golden horseshoe.

Vegas Vic
This towering neon cowboy with the flickering cigarette at the Pioneer Club, 25 Fremont Street, is one of the

most photographed signs in Las Vegas. Built in 1951 by the Young Electric Sign Company, it was designed as a glittering blow-up of the "Howdy Pardner" trademark used by the Las Vegas Chamber of Commerce. Over the years, Vegas Vic has become a symbol of the city on countless travel brochures and book covers.

The Post Office/Federal Building

Listed on the National Register of Historic Places, this structure at 301 East Stewart Street is a legacy of the massive building program launched by the Herbert Hoover administration in the 1930s. When it was completed in 1933, the neoclassical post office housed the U.S. District Courts.

Las Vegas High School

Another Hoover-era building on the National Register, the high school, located at 315 South Seventh Street, dates back to 1931. In a neighborhood of mission-style architecture, this building stands out with its art deco facade. Notice the heroic sculptured figures above the doors and the ornate flowers and animals everywhere you look. Clark County historians say it's the only art deco building in town.

Las Vegas Hospital

This was considered a very modern medical center in 1931, when it was built for a group of doctors. It's empty now, but the old adobe structure at 201 North Eighth Street was used as a hospital until the 1960s and was later converted into a drug rehabilitation center.

Masonic Lodge

Tucked away at 213 South Third Street, this mission-style building was built in 1936 as headquarters for the local Masons fraternal group. It is now the Clark County Law Library.

The Smith House

A showplace when it was completed in 1932 for Dr. J. D. Smith, a prosperous dentist and civic leader, the home is now on the National Register of Historic Places. Located at 624 South Sixth Street, six blocks south of Fremont and three blocks east of the railroad bungalows, the Smith house was once in a fashionable neighborhood of ambitious homes. Now restored by the Smith family, the rambling old house is occupied by professional offices.

If you're fascinated by old houses, you'll find others in the same neighborhood. For a quick history lesson, pick up a copy of *A Guide to Historic Las Vegas,* a compact brochure compiled by the Preservation Association of Clark County. It traces the area's history since 1844 and lists twenty-four significant landmarks. Pick up a free copy of the brochure, which includes a map, at museums and tourist information counters, or you may call the Nevada State Museum and Historical Society at (702) 385-0115. For more historical information, write to the Preservation Association of Clark County, P.O. Box 96686, Las Vegas, NV 89193-6686.

MORE HISTORY... EVEN EARLIER

How far back shall we go? In later chapters, we'll explore some outlying places known by the Indians in ancient times, but the city proper traces its specific origins to John Fremont's 1844 report of his visit to the watering place in the meadow called Las Vegas. If you're sightseeing downtown by car, pick up the freeway (U.S.

Highway 95) at Las Vegas Boulevard, just north of City Hall, and go west into history. Turn off at Valley View Boulevard and head south to Alta Drive. Now you're in the neighborhood of Fremont's Big Springs.

The Las Vegas Valley Water District
3701 West Alta Drive
Open Monday–Friday, 8 A.M. to 4:30 P.M.
Admission is free; for more information call
(702) 258-3205

The Big Spring where Fremont and his party quenched their thirst 150 years ago is the number one attraction here, listed on the National Register of Historic Places. Actually, there are several springs on this spot. They provided all the water for the Las Vegas valley until Lake Mead began to supply the city in the 1950s. Now the Water District has opened **Desert Demonstration Gardens**, displaying more than 180 different varieties of plants in eleven different theme areas.

On the other side of the freeway, you'll find two museums and a scenic lake in **Lorenzi Park**. (A warning worth repeating: You can't see everything in one day; make your choice from the menu.)

From the Water District gardens, go back to Valley View and head north to West Washington Avenue. Turn right on Washington and you're almost there. At Twin Lakes Drive, turn right again and you'll come to the entrance of the State Museum. Here's where those unassembled fragments of Las Vegas history are brought together into a coherent picture.

Nevada State Museum and Historical Society
700 Twin Lakes Drive
Open daily, 9 A.M. to 5 P.M.
Call for information about tours, exhibits, lectures, and public programs: (702) 486-5205

This rambling Spanish colonial-style building is southern Nevada's only nationally accredited museum. Permanent exhibits trace the region's growth from ancient Indian cultures to Spanish exploration and later Mormon settlements, to the railroad builders, to modern times. In the Hall of Biology, you learn about the natural history of southern Nevada and the plants and animals living in the region. The Hall of Regional History displays photos and documents recalling the past, including the days of mining, nuclear bomb testing, and the building of Hoover Dam. Changing exhibits focus on cultural developments, arts, and sciences. The Cahlan Library stores historical documents, newspaper indexes, and reference materials about Nevada. The museum closes only on Thanksgiving, Christmas, and New Year's Day.

Las Vegas Art Museum
3333 West Washington Avenue (in Lorenzi Park)
Open Tuesday–Saturday, 10 A.M. to 3 P.M.;
Sunday, noon to 3 P.M.
Call for exhibit information: (702) 647-4300

Across the lake from the State Museum and Historical Society, the Las Vegas Art Museum occupies two modest one-story buildings. Originally, the structures were part of Twin Lakes Lodge Resort, a popular vacation spot for politicians and Hollywood stars in the 1940s. The city of Las Vegas bought the resort and surrounding land in 1965 and created Lorenzi Park on eighty acres.

The art collection in this museum is not huge, but exhibits in three galleries change monthly. The Main Gallery displays works by nationally and internationally known painters and sculptors. The Nevada Gallery showcases regional artists, and the Mini Gallery presents art auctions. In the museum studios, visiting artists offer special workshops from time to time, and local artists teach year-round classes for children and adults. A recent addition is the Youth Gallery, where young artists show their work. A gift shop offers original art at reasonable prices.

Southern Nevada Zoological Society
1775 North Rancho Drive
Open daily, 9 A.M. to 5 P.M.
(702) 648-5955

It's small and friendly—a four-acre zoo and botanical garden with an assortment of African, Asian, and American animals. Some are on loan from the San Diego Zoo. Popular favorites include a cougar who grew up in human company after being rescued in 1988 from a roadside near Elko, Nevada, after his mother was killed by a car. Kids who love animals will find new friends in the petting zoo. And if Ronald Raven is still there to greet them, they'll remember the "talking bird" long after your Las Vegas vacation is over. Getting there is easy from Lorenzi Park: Go east on Washington Avenue to Rancho Drive and turn north.

A SMORGASBORD OF MUSEUMS

The variety of museums in Las Vegas often surprises adventurous visitors who set out to see more than the famous pleasure palaces on the Strip. One of these museums was designed and built especially for children. Many others feature special exhibits for children.

If you're ready for more sight-seeing when you leave the zoo, drive back to Washington and head east to another cluster of museums near the intersection of East Washington and Las Vegas Boulevard. Better still, make this a separate daytrip; you'll enjoy it more if you start when you're feeling fresh and full of energy.

History and archaeology buffs will want to visit the **Old Mormon Fort**, the earliest settlement in the Las Vegas valley. Next door, budding naturalists will find hands-on fun and live sharks at the **Las Vegas Natural History Museum**. And, for youngsters, the best museum of all is the **Lied Discovery Children's Museum** across the street. We'll begin with the oldest, but you and your family will decide where *you* want to start.

> **Old Las Vegas Mormon Fort**
> **State Historic Park**
> 908 Las Vegas Boulevard North
> Hours vary with the season
> Admission is free; for more information call
> (702) 486-3511

The oldest building in Las Vegas is a tiny adobe remnant, the last remaining fragment of a fort built in 1855 by a Mormon settlement company. The missionaries had been appointed by Brigham Young to establish a halfway station between Utah and California and to bring the gospel to the Indians. They didn't stay long. Less than three years later, the Mormons were on their way. Ranchers moved in, and this little building became a storage shed on the Las Vegas ranch. Later on, when the railroad took over the ranchland, it leased the Old Fort buildings to a series of tenants, including government researchers who used the small shed in the early 1930s for testing concrete used in the Hoover Dam. In those days, more of the original buildings were still standing.

Daughters of Utah Pioneers (DUP) in Las Vegas kept an eye on the Old Fort during World War II. They leased it from the railroad and set out to preserve what was left. But in 1955, the railroad sold the property to Elks

Lodge #1468, and a restaurant signed a lease on the ranch house. The DUP still protected the small adobe remnant, but the Elks demolished the other buildings in 1963. The City of Las Vegas bought the little shed in 1971 and entered it on the National Register of Historic Places the following year. Various preservation groups took care of it until 1991, when the state of Nevada bought the Old Fort site and 2.75 acres of land around it.

Now the Old Fort is a state historic park under the Nevada Division of State Parks. Since December 1994, archaeologists have been digging systematically, mapping the original foundations of the fort and ranch buildings. Supporters hope eventually to reconstruct the Old Fort. Visitors are welcome now, but museum hours may change. Call before you go. For more details call the museum or Nevada State Parks, District 6, at (702) 486-5126.

Las Vegas Natural History Museum
900 Las Vegas Boulevard North
Open daily, 9 A.M. to 4 P.M.
Call for more information: (702) 384-3466; ask about
Thursday lectures and feeding time for the sharks

It may seem small to children who have seen the Smithsonian in Washington, D.C., the Field Museum in Chicago, or the Museum of Natural History in New York, but this is a very friendly little museum. The Young Scientist Center is a favorite with visitors of all ages who like hands-on exhibits, video games, and puzzles with a purpose. Toddlers can ride toy animals or play in the fossil sandbox. Animals are the main attraction in other rooms.

The International Wildlife Room displays big animals from around the world—wolves, bears, bison, and big cats like tigers and leopards—all preserved by taxidermy.

A Dinosaur Den has three very lifelike animated dinosaurs, along with real dinosaur skeletons and fossils of other prehistoric animals. The Marine Life Room has live sharks swimming in a small tank and shows videos of sharks at home in the sea. A snake exhibit explodes some myths about rattlesnakes and sidewinders; and the new Wild Nevada Room displays animals and plants of southern Nevada. Out in the main hallway, an art gallery exhibits wood carvings of wildlife. To learn more, attend one of the lectures every third Thursday.

The Natural History Museum and the Old Mormon Fort are close to each other at the edge of the Cashman Field Center. On the other side of Las Vegas Boulevard, you'll see the spacious **Las Vegas Library** and, next door to it, a museum designed with children in mind. Plan ahead for this one. With kids of any age, you'll want to spend a whole morning or afternoon here, even if you have to skip the other museums.

Lied Discovery Children's Museum

833 Las Vegas Boulevard North
Open Tuesday–Saturday, 10 A.M. to 5 P.M.;
Wednesday, 10 A.M. to 7 P.M.; Sunday, noon to 5 P.M.
(702) 382-5437
Admission: adults $5.00; students, seniors, military
$4.00; children 3–11 $3.00; members and children
under 2 are free.

Any child can make a test run through life in the Everyday Living Section, where you choose a career, get a job, receive a paycheck, deposit it in the bank, and withdraw funds (in play money) from an automatic teller machine. Go next door to the General Store and see how far the cash will stretch. In the Hospital, you can treat a patient or *be* a patient. Or you might be an actor on the Performing Arts stage or a disc jockey at

KKID radio. If you want to be a broadcaster, painter, musician, astronaut, or computer scientist, there's a place for you here.

Inside the eight-story Science Tower, you can bend sound waves in the Echo Tubes or create a fantastic light show with the neon and fiber-optics display. The Periscope gives you a camera view of the whole Las Vegas valley, and the Weather Computer relays information from the instruments mounted on top of the tower. In another room, at Toddler Towers, the stroller set can play with soft toys and crawl and slide in carpeted comfort.

There's a snack bar for lunch and a special room for birthday parties. The gift shop has affordable trinkets and educational games and kits. Phone ahead to find out about seasonal exhibits, demonstrations, and performances.

THE UNIVERSITY OF NEVADA, LAS VEGAS

You're not through exploring the "other" Las Vegas until you've seen the University of Nevada campus, where nearly twenty-thousand students attend classes. Some pursue traditional degrees in arts and sciences, but many come here to study hotel management, performing arts, or the economics of gaming and entertainment. Part-time jobs on the Strip give them firsthand experience. Student archaeologists and paleontologists don't just examine prehistoric fossils, they uncover them in the neighboring desert.

University of Nevada, Las Vegas
4505 South Maryland Parkway
(702) 895-3381; for campus tours, call (702) 895-3443

There are no ivy-covered brick buildings—all the structures are less than forty years old—yet there's a comfortable feeling of quiet permanence mixed with the youthful vigor of this 335-acre campus. Tree-shaded walks lead from one modern building to the next. The oldest structure, Maude Frazier Hall, opened in 1957 as headquarters for Nevada Southern University. Twelve years later, the school was renamed after becoming part of the University of Nevada system, along with the much older University of Nevada in Reno.

Guided tours of the campus can be arranged through the admissions office by calling (702) 895-3443 or by just dropping by: Maude Frazier Hall, Room 114. If you'd rather find your way around by yourselves, ask for a campus map. A few highlights are worth special attention.

Marjorie Barrick Museum of Natural History

Harmon Avenue at Gym Road
Open Monday–Friday, 9 A.M. to 5 P.M.;
Saturday, 10 A.M. to 5 P.M.
Admission is free; for more information call
(702) 895-3381

More ambitious than the Las Vegas Natural History Museum, this one adds an outdoor botanical garden and permanent indoor exhibits, examining the geology, biology, and archaeology of the desert. You'll see animals and insects, big snakes and lizards, spiders and beetles—anything that lives in the Mojave Desert. The endangered desert tortoise rates a special display. And the first thing you'll notice is the huge reconstructed skeleton of an ichthyosaur, a prehistoric sea lizard that is Nevada's state fossil. (How many other states have official fossils?)

Center for the Performing Arts
North end of Academic Mall
Call for ticket prices and schedules: (702) 895-3801

Opera, ballet, chamber music, and pop concerts take turns on the stages of the **Artemus W. Ham Concert Hall** and the **Judy Bayley Theatre** in this two-part complex. If you're in Las Vegas between September and April, phone for schedules and ticket information. Between October and May, the center is home to the Nevada Dance Theatre. One phone number reaches the box office for both facilities.

In case you're wondering about that avant-garde, thirty-eight-foot steel sculpture in the plaza outside the center, it's called *Flashlight* and is the work of Claes Oldenberg and Coosje van Bruggen.

Donna Beam Fine Art Gallery
Ham Fine Arts Building, Room 130
Open Monday–Friday, 8 A.M. to 5 P.M.
(702) 895-3893

See changing exhibitions of work by students, faculty, and invited artists. Admission is free.

Thomas and Mack Center
Call for ticket prices and schedules: (702) 895-3900

Basketball fans fill the 18,500 seats of this indoor arena to watch the UNLV "Runnin' Rebels" play home games during the winter season, December through February. The rest of the time, it's used for concerts, shows, and sporting events.

Silver Bowl Regional Park
Off U.S. Highway 93/95, Russell Road exit
(702) 895-3900

Not on campus, but very much a part of the UNLV scene in football season, September through November. The **Sam Boyd Silver Bowl** is also used for summer concerts and year-round sports competitions.

ONLY IN LAS VEGAS...

If you need a reminder that you're in the glitter capital of the world, take a look at the list of entertainment museums in the Las Vegas Yellow Pages. You know about the ones on the Strip, but have you heard of the Elvis Elvis Elvis Museum of Elvis Mementos or the World Boxing Hall of Champions or Bethany's Celebrity Doll Museum? They're all listed at the same address and telephone number, but all seem to have disappeared since the 1994 phone book went to press. Such enterprises come and go, but one entertainment museum has grown into such a successful tourist attraction that it ranks ahead of everything else in the area—except the casinos, Hoover Dam, and Lake Mead. It's a few blocks east of the Strip, beyond the Maryland Parkway, but easy to find. Just look for busloads of tourists in the parking lot.

The Liberace Museum
1775 East Tropicana Avenue
Open Monday–Saturday, 10 A.M. to 5 P.M.;
Sunday, 1 P.M. to 5 P.M.
(702) 798-5595 or (800) 626-2625
Admission: adults $6.50; seniors $4.50; students $3.50; children 6–12 $2; children under 6 are free.

Where else would you find such a tribute to an outrageous entertainer? For years Liberace attracted thousands of fans to his live performances and millions of viewers to broadcasts of his television show. He was "Mister Showmanship" and "Mister Las Vegas." Women fainted, so the story goes, when he came on stage in one of his flamboyant sequin-and-rhinestone costumes. The ornate candelabra on his grand piano became his trademark.

At this museum dedicated to Liberace's memory, you learn that he was born Walter Valentino Liberace on May 16, 1919. He had his name legally changed in 1950 to simply "Liberace." Before becoming an entertainment legend, he had been a prodigy pianist at age seven in his native Wisconsin and a concert performer at fourteen. He first played in Las Vegas in the old days, when he was just twenty-three. As the city grew more and more flashy, so did Liberace.

The museum preserves some of his more spectacular costumes, including lavish fur capes, and suits decorated with ostrich feathers, bugle beads, and rhinestones. You'll also see "the world's biggest rhinestone," fifty pounds of sparkle worth $50,000, and an ornately decorated rolltop desk from the entertainer's office. All that is in the main building. There's more.

Across the parking lot, in the piano and car gallery, Liberace's custom-made rhinestone car with its matching toolbox is displayed along with his mirror-tiled Rolls Royce and more cars. There's a collection of rare pianos, including a concert grand once owned by George Gershwin, and an antique instrument reputedly played by Frederic Chopin, both of which are outglitzed by Liberace's own rhinestone-studded Baldwin piano. A separate library building contains his gold records, family photos, historical information, and collections of miniature pianos, silver, china, and crystal.

In the gift shop, you can buy a Liberace doll for $300 or a copy of his autobiography for $30. Of course there are Liberace record albums, songbooks, tapes, photos, and postcards. The museum is open every day of the year except Thanksgiving, Christmas, and New Year's Day.

CHAPTER 7

And Now, a Little Shopping...

Whether it's aspirin you need or a diamond bracelet, you'll find it in Las Vegas if you know where to look. Shopping is inevitable in this city—part of the entertainment—even if you don't buy anything.

From the moment you step out of the elevator in your hotel, you'll see things to buy. Be warned! Some children will find temptations at every turn. Adults with money in their pockets will be targets for some very fancy sales strategies.

If you call it "shopping" when you buy a toothbrush, you'll probably stick to your budget in Las Vegas. But if you're an impulse buyer, tempted by glittering window displays of designer clothes and rhinestone-studded shoes, maybe you'd better put a padlock on your wallet.

Now, what do you want to buy? The morning newspaper is as close as the little shop in your hotel lobby. So are necessities such as shaving cream, cough drops, peanuts, and postcards. The same shops will inevitably have a stock of souvenirs stamped with a local logo.

Some resorts and casino-hotels have shopping arcades or rows of boutiques, displaying luxury clothes and jewelry, plush toys, and expensive works of art. If you're staying at one of the major resorts, you'll find these show-places soon after you arrive. One of the first things you'll notice in most of them is multidigit price tags. There may be a store or two in the group in which moderate prices are visible on T-shirts, caps, small toys, and mementos.

For practical shopping in department stores and spe-cialty shops, explore the city's retail malls. Las Vegas has some big ones with tenant names you'll recognize. For name-brand bargains, try one of the factory outlet malls south of the Strip. And don't overlook the shops at museums and visitor centers at outdoor recreation areas. Most of these have small items priced to fit a child's allowance.

RETAIL SHOPPING MALLS

Without leaving the Las Vegas Strip, you can visit two of the city's most luxurious shopping malls. Both are centrally located, near all the attractions between Flamingo and Desert Inn Roads. One is built around five department stores and scores of smaller shops. The other is an enter-tainment experience not to be missed, whether you plan to buy an ice cream cone, a teddy bear, or a $1,500 maribou-trimmed negligee—The Forum Shops at Caesars Palace.

The Forum Shops at Caesars
3570 Las Vegas Boulevard South
Open daily, 10 A.M. to 11 P.M.

The weather is always balmy inside this fantasy mall. Even the golden afternoon light seems Mediterranean. Wispy white clouds drift overhead against a painted sky. When it's dark outside in the real world, this indoor sky changes from pale blue to pinkish dusk to deep azure sprinkled with stars.

You stroll along Roman roads, past ornate fountains and frescoed facades of classic buildings with very modern store windows. Specialty shops like **Kids Kastle**, **Sungear**, **Brookstone**, **Victoria's Secret**, and **Express Compagnie Internationale** share the scene with such designer stores as **Gucci**, **Louis Vuitton**, **Gianni Versace**, **Gabrielli**, and **Bernini**.

Families with children head straight for the Festival Fountain. (If they haven't been told what's about to happen, they follow the crowds out of curiosity.) In a piazza defined by Roman columns and arches, a towering statue of Bacchus, the Roman god of merriment and wine, smiles benevolently from his throne at the center of the fountain. Companion statues of Venus, Apollo, and Plutus surround him, like figures on a giant wedding cake, in a lighted pool fed by arching streams of water.

Every hour the sound of thunder heralds the start of a seven-minute spectacle. As lightning flashes in the domed sky above the fountain, statues "come to life," opening their electronically automated eyes and speaking to the crowd. Apollo provides music with his lyre; Venus offers appropriate greetings. Plutus, Roman god of wealth, calls up cascades of colored lights in the computer-controlled waterscape. For a finale, Bacchus summons Apollo's chariot of the sun. Through the magic of laser light and other special effects, the chariot rolls across the sky while mythical images appear in the dancing waters.

At the end of this brief show, music, water, and lights subside, and the statues are again just statues. Shoppers resume their explorations of the Roman streetscape, discovering more stores and restaurants. Some may stop at a coffee bar for cappucino and biscotti. Others buy ice-cream cones to eat as they stroll. Those ready for a full meal can choose from an assortment of possibilities.

If you're too hungry to wait in a long line outside **Planet Hollywood**, keep walking. You'll find a variety of menus at Wolfgang Puck's **Spago, Boogie's Diner of Aspen, The Palm, La Salsa, Swensen's Ice Cream Parlor,** and the **Stage Deli.** At **Bertolini's,** you'll imagine you're on the Via Veneto as you dine "outdoors" in the central piazza beside the Fountain of the Gods.

Need a little vigorous exercise? **Just for Feet,** the athletic-shoe store, has treadmill machines and a half-sized basketball court, where you can test the shoes you buy. An occasional sports celebrity may turn up to sign autographs.

At **Warner Brothers Studios Store**, visitors can watch cartoons and movie clips on a big video wall or sit down in the discovery area and learn how to make their own cartoons.

Magic Masters entices you into a replica of Harry Houdini's private library to watch mystifying demonstrations. Amateur wizards who decide to buy equipment here will be escorted through a secret door to learn how to perform their illusions.

The Museum Company gives you a chance to shop at museums around the world without leaving the Forum. Cards and gifts from the Boston Museum and the Smithsonian in Washington, D.C., are displayed, along with items from London's Tate Gallery and the Louvre in Paris, to name a few.

Children love to browse at **Endangered Species**, a nature store offering books, tapes, puzzles, games, stuffed animals, and educational toys. The shop has some inexpensive mementos too.

And there's more. Such names as **Ann Taylor**, **Guess**, **Cache**, **Bulgari**, and **Zero Gravity** identify individual stores. For a complete list, pick up a brochure at the mall entrance.

The Forum Shops adjoin Caesars Palace, but the mall was developed jointly by Melvin Simon & Associates of Indianapolis and the Gordon Company of Los Angeles, with the cooperation of Henry Gluck, chairman of Caesars World, Inc. The partners brought in Dougall Designs of Los Angeles to create an extravagant interior with a Roman theme.

Principal designer Terry Dougall says he imagined the mall as a theater setting, carrying shoppers through two thousand years of Roman history, from about 300 B.C. to A.D. 1700. Every detail of the decor had to be historically accurate. Dougall researchers spent weeks consulting historical records for information about building materials, colors, and decorations of the period.

"If I couldn't document it, we wouldn't do it," Dougall said.

Since The Forum Shops opened at Caesars in 1992, the mall has been managed by Simon & Associates, owner-managers of more than 140 shopping centers in thirty states, including the giant Mall of America in Bloomington, Minnesota.

From Las Vegas Boulevard, you enter The Forum Shops on a moving sidewalk that starts just outside the Mirage. Caesars "people movers" travel in one direction only, so you have to find another way out through the casino. Confusing, but ask directions from one of the costumed centurions near the bottom of the escalator.

Fashion Show Mall
3200 Las Vegas Boulevard South
Open Monday–Friday, 10 A.M. to 9 P.M.;
Saturday, 10 A.M. to 7 P.M.; Sunday, noon to 6 P.M.

A block away from Caesars, across Spring Mountain Road from Treasure Island, the Fashion Show Mall on the Strip attracts local shoppers and visitors to five big department stores and at least 140 other tenants. Walk through upscale **Neiman Marcus** to reach central passageways leading to **Bullock's**, **Saks Fifth Avenue**, **Dillard's**, and **Robinson's-May**. Each of these anchor stores is flanked by rows of specialty shops and boutiques on two levels connected by escalators.

Abercrombie & Fitch, **Banana Republic**, **Benetton**, **Casual Corner**, **The Limited**, **Talbot's**, and **Victoria's Secret** are just a few of the familiar names you'll find in the mall. Readers gravitate to **Waldenbooks**, seeking literary classics, current bestsellers, and magazines. There are fifteen shoe stores, nine jewelers, two art galleries, and nine places for toys, gifts, and cards.

For children's clothes, look into **Animal Crackers** and **Brats**, as well as the five department stores. If your kids find **The Disney Store**, be prepared to stay for a while and walk out with a package or two.

Small women find their sizes at **Petite Sophisticates** and the **5-7-9** store; big women go to **Lane Bryant** and **Bullock's Woman**. Men aren't neglected at **Harris & Frank**, **Custom Shop Shirtmakers**, **Schwartz Big and Tall**, **Oak Tree**, **Uomo-Uomo Sport**, and **Zeidler**

& Zeidler. A dozen unisex shops supply jeans and sports togs for Mom and Dad.

A food court, near Robinson's-May on the street level, offers international fast food at fifteen booths, including **Aloha Teriyaki**, **Burger Express**, **Renzio's Greek Food**, **Yang's Wok**, and **Dairy Queen**. For a more leisurely lunch or dinner, try **Morton's of Chicago**, a steakhouse on the second level, directly above the food court.

If you have a prescription to be filled or just need shampoo and cough syrup, the **Omni Chemist** has licensed pharmacists and the usual drugstore items, from hair dryers to eyedrops.

Like most big-city malls, Fashion Show has an automatic teller machine and a customer service desk to provide general information, bus schedules, and show tickets. You can borrow a stroller or wheelchair if you leave a piece of identification on deposit until you return it. This mall also offers valet parking and a $10 car wash from 10 A.M. to 2 P.M., Wednesday through Saturday.

Dedicated shoppers who have time to leave the Strip can reach other malls in the city by bus, taxi, or car. These spacious hunting grounds are much more down-to-earth than The Forum Shops at Caesars, but you'll still find plenty of glitz.

The Boulevard Mall
3528 South Maryland Parkway
Open Monday–Friday, 10 A.M. to 9 P.M.; Saturday,
10 A.M. to 7 P.M.; Sunday, 11 A.M. to 6 P.M.

Covering more than a million square feet, the Boulevard Mall is Nevada's largest shopping mall, recently expanded after twenty-six years as a local shopping mecca. Anchor stores are **J.C. Penney**, **Sears**, and **Broadway Southwest**.

Sunlight filters through the arched glass ceiling above landscaped avenues of shops. You might almost imagine you're in an outdoor garden, but controlled air-conditioning protects you from sizzling summer heat.

Boulevard specialty shops include **The Nature Company**, **Sesame Street General Store**, **Traders West**, **Sanrio Surprises**, **Charlotte Russe**, and at least a hundred more. Visit the food court for a snack or a meal.

A taxi will get you there in a hurry, or you can park in the covered garage. Valet parking is available.

The Meadows Mall
4300 Meadows Lane
Open Monday–Friday, 10 A.M. to 9 P.M.;
Saturday–Sunday, 10 A.M. to 6 P.M.

Just off U.S. Highway 95 at Valley View Boulevard, this enclosed shopping center is a ten-minute cab ride from most hotels on the Strip. The mall also provides its own trolley from the Downtown Transportation Center at Stewart Avenue and Casino Center Boulevard.

The Meadows Mall offers some of the same stores found in the other malls. Four department stores, **Dillard's**, **Broadway**, **J.C. Penney's**, and **Sears**, share space with more than 135 smaller shops on two levels. Avenues of specialty stores and restaurants zigzag through five courtyards.

Chinatown Plaza
4155 Spring Mountain Road
Open daily, 10 A.M. to 10 P.M.

Just a mile west of Treasure Island, a yellow-tiled roof with distinctive curves guides you to an Oriental adventure. This brand-new shopping center, opened for Christmas 1994, is still expanding. The anchor store is a big supermarket—fourteen thousand square feet—stocked with Asian delicacies and ingredients. Inside the mall, a sculptured centerpiece recalls folktales of the mischievous Monkey God, chasing demons with his bamboo cane.

Eight restaurants, some open as late as 4 A.M., serve Oriental specialties such as Korean barbecue, Japanese sushi, Vietnamese noodles, and Cantonese dim sum. Shops are brimming with exotic imports, from Japanese lacquer to Chinese embroidery. With lucky timing, you may see a wedding party emerge from the chapel, where a robed monk performs traditional marriage ceremonies.

FACTORY OUTLET MALLS

All over the country, name-brand manufacturers are opening outlet stores, selling overstock merchandise at discount prices. Some offer savings of 20 to 70 percent. You've seen them in your area: sprawling labyrinths or smaller groups of stores, usually located near a freeway exit.

If bargain hunting is part of your Las Vegas vacation, head south on the Strip. You'll find two large factory outlet centers. The first is about three miles south of the Hacienda Hotel, on the left. The second is two miles farther, on the right. Both can be reached by CAT (Citizens Area Transit) bus or, of course, by taxi.

Belz Factory Outlet World
Las Vegas Boulevard South, at Warm Springs Road
Open Monday–Saturday, 10 A.M. to 9 P.M.; Sunday,
10 A.M. to 6 P.M.

Inside a climate-controlled mall built on thirty-six acres of former desert, some seventy outlet shops cover 250,000 square feet. A permanent laser light show entertains children and parents. A food court provides meals and snacks.

About half of the stores in this mall are clothing outlets with instantly recognizable names, such as **Carter's Childrenswear, Oshkosh B'Gosh, Danskin, Nike, Adolfo II**, and **Ducks Unlimited**. Mixed in with these are fragrance outlets, a book warehouse, accessory shops, toys, housewares, jewelers, and shoe stores.

Nonsmokers will appreciate the unpolluted air; Belz Factory Outlet World is one of the few facilities in Las Vegas with a no-smoking policy.

Factory Stores of America
(Formerly, Las Vegas Factory Stores)
9155 Las Vegas Boulevard South
Open Monday–Saturday, 10 A.M. to 8 P.M.; Sunday, 10 A.M. to 6 P.M.

Down the road from the Belz mall, this recently expanded shopping center has some fifty stores offering manufacturers' discounts. In a landscaped outdoor setting on thirty acres, Spanish-style buildings house factory stores for such well-known labels as **Geoffrey Beene, Izod, Van Heusen**, and **Florsheim**. Kids will want to browse at **Toy Liquidators**. Housewares shoppers will find sheets, towels, bedspreads, and the like at **West Point Pepperell**, and fine china and kitchen equipment at **Mikasa**. Luggage bargains can be found at **American Tourister**.

Out-of-state visitors, surprised to find slot machines in Nevada supermarkets and Laundromats (even the airports!), can take home one more story about the Wild West: When Las Vegas Factory Stores expanded, developers added the **Outlet Lounge**, a bar patterned after a sports casino, complete with video poker and slot machines.

COWBOY BOOTS AND
OTHER WESTERN GEAR

Much of Nevada is still cattle country. Real cowboys on the range still outnumber rhinestone cowboys on the Strip. Travelers eager to take home authentic souvenirs of the Old West can consult the Las Vegas Yellow Pages for a list of western-wear stores. The shopping section of *What's On in Las Vegas,* a free magazine distributed in hotels, may also offer suggestions. Here are a few easy-to-find western stores.

Cowtown Boots
2989 Paradise Road, across from the Convention Center
Open Monday–Saturday, 10 A.M. to 8 P.M.;
Sunday, noon to 5 P.M.

Even toddlers can find boots to fit at this western store, as can their moms and dads. Handmade boots are a specialty, but that's not all. From bandanas and bola ties to western shirts and jeans, you can outfit the whole family or surprise someone with a gift.

Tumbleweed Western Wear
4213 Las Vegas Boulevard South, at the Fez Motel
Open Tuesday–Saturday, 10 A.M. to 6 P.M.

Try on a cowboy hat or a square-dance skirt. Kids who love cowboy movies and TV shows can costume themselves for favorite roles. Here's where some country-western performers and their fans find those exotic-patterned boots with high heels and pointed toes. Big, tall cowboys will find extra-large shirts and boots. **Justin**, **Tony Lama**, **Panhandle Slim**, and **Wrangler** are just a few name brands in stock. **Stetson** hats, too.

Western Emporium
5111 Boulder Highway (outside entrance at
Sam's Town)
Open Sunday–Thursday, 9 A.M. to 10 P.M.;
Friday–Saturday, 9 A.M. to midnight

All the well-known brand labels on shirts, boots, and
hats can be found here. Also jewelry, original art, and
gourmet coffees.

ART GALLERIES

Some travelers hunt for art treasures wherever they go.
If your favorite souvenir is something to hang on the
wall or display on a curio shelf, you'll spend some time
browsing in art shops. Here are a few conveniently
located galleries.

Art Encounter
3979 West Spring Mountain Road
Phone for current schedule: (702) 227-0220

The city's largest art gallery exhibits the work of local
and national artists: oils, watercolors, sculpture, and jewelry. The gallery claims to display about two thousand
works by at least a hundred artists at one time. Sometimes you'll see artists at work during business hours.

Moonstruck Gallery
6322 West Sahara Avenue
(702) 364-0531 or (800) 421-9133

Lots of variety here. Disney animation art and limited-
edition prints are specialties, but there's more. You'll
find handcrafted musical instruments, hand-blown
glass, kaleidoscopes, jewelry, and pottery.

Elk Dreamer Gallery
2240 Paradise Road
(702) 735-4104

Originals, limited editions, and prints are on display, along with unusual bronze jewelry. The gallery does framing too, and will ship your gifts for you.

Deborah Spanover Fine Arts
1775 East Tropicana Avenue, Suite 21–22
(702) 739-0072; Fax: 739-9720

If you're an art dealer, phone for an appointment. Spanover sells sculptures, limited-edition prints, and original works, wholesale and retail.

Boulder City Art Guild and Gallery
1496 Nevada Highway, Boulder City
Open Tuesday–Sunday, noon to 4 P.M.
(702) 293-2138

If you're in the mood for some art browsing on your way to Hoover Dam, stop off in Boulder City and take a look at the work of local artists.

And There's More . . .

New shops and malls seem to spring up overnight in Las Vegas. By the time you've read this far, there's probably more, including a new fourteen-acre shopping center with canopied walkways on Maryland Parkway, near the big Boulevard Mall. We haven't even begun to explore the variety of small shops in the city. You'll find some of those as you set out on your own.

CHAPTER 8

International Influences

Scottish bagpipers share the spotlight with Thai dancers and Ethiopian musicians. A Mexican *folklorico* group ends its performance and makes room for an energetic Hawaiian hula. The silver melody from a Paraguayan harp yields to the beat of Native American drums and joyous shouts from an African American gospel choir.

At the annual **Las Vegas Folklife Festival** in Lorenzi Park, the atmosphere is always international. Spicy aromas attract you to food booths selling traditional dishes from India, Japan, Greece, Lithuania, and who-knows-what other exotic spots around the world. Craft demonstrations draw you to work areas, where a Navajo silversmith deftly shapes a belt buckle, Ukrainian artists paint elaborate Easter eggs, African American quilters display their handiwork, and a Filipino craftsman perfects a multicolored kite. On stage in the Sammy Davis Jr. Memorial Plaza, a swirl of costumes provides a round-the-world tour.

Once a year, usually in April, Las Vegas celebrates its cultural diversity with a festival organized by the Nevada State Council on the Arts. Anytime you visit the city, you'll be aware of this ethnic mix. Street names, restaurant menus, and shops reflect cosmopolitan influences on a town that was once typically Old West.

From the moment you land at the airport, you'll see faces from every corner of the globe: Hispanic, Asian, African, East Indian, and Pacific Islander types along with Europeans and Native Americans. Some of these faces belong to visitors like yourself, but the people who live and work here also represent a potpourri of origins.

Since the first Spanish surveyors gave the valley its name more than two centuries ago, Las Vegas has attracted travelers. Long before that, a thousand years before European pioneers drank from the Big Springs, the valley was familiar territory to the Anasazi—"the Ancient Ones." These early visitors belonged to an assortment of nomadic native tribes, all speaking different languages or dialects. Over the centuries, some of them settled here for a while before moving on. When the first white men arrived in the valley, they found a Paiute camp near the Big Springs, with a few cone-shaped shelters surrounded by patches of squash, corn, sunflowers, and pumpkins. Since then these native people have left their indelible imprint on the city that grew up around their early camps.

THE FIRST LAS VEGANS

Descendants of the ancient tribes are now called Native Americans of the Great Basin (Nevada, Utah, Idaho, Wyoming, and California) and are recognized by the state of Nevada as having sovereign independent governments. Northern and Southern Paiute, Washoe, Shoshone, and Goshute tribes occupy reservations and colonies scattered across Nevada's Indian Territory. Southern Paiutes were the first people to put down permanent roots in the Las Vegas valley.

As white settlers moved in, Paiutes were gradually outnumbered and pushed out of the valley. A few stayed in the area, and some worked for the whites as ranch hands and house servants. Others found jobs with the railroad and with mines that sprang up in the surrounding desert.

Eventually, in 1912, the Las Vegas Paiutes were given legal title to ten acres of desert on what was left of the Las Vegas Ranch after the San Pedro–Los Angeles–Salt Lake Railroad had bought the rest. Today those ten acres, inside the Las Vegas city limits, are still a Paiute colony with its own separate local government. Now the tribe is developing a much larger community on thirty-seven hundred acres north of the city, west of U.S. Highway 95. Travelers on that road are watching the gradual transformation of an industrial site, where a Paiute company, Nuwuvi Composites Technologies, manufactures aerospace components. There's plenty of undeveloped land around the plant, and the tribe's master plan is ambitious.

On the drawing board is a residential community for aerospace workers, and a resort with hotels, casinos, and four public championship golf courses with views of Mount Charleston. Early in 1995, golfers were strolling across the greens and hitting balls on the first of these courses (see chapter 9).

Such plans would have been impossible for Las Vegas Paiutes in earlier times. As recently as the 1950s, with their tiny colony completely surrounded by the growing city, the tribe fought and defeated attempts by city developers to buy their ten acres. Until 1962 they had no city water or sewer services. Finally, in 1968, the federal government's Indians Claims Commission approved an $8 million settlement to compensate for lands taken from Southern Pauites. Part of this money went to the Las Vegas tribe.

In the 1990s, Clark County has become a crossroads of tribal cultures, with the largest Native American population of any county in Nevada. Of the 19,634 urban Indians in the state, according to a recent census, more than half live in Clark County. An estimated 98 percent of these do not live on reservations; they're simply part of the Las Vegas/Clark County community.

"They've come here from almost every tribe in North America, from Alaska to New York," said Richard Arnold, executive director of the Las Vegas Indian Center. "For example, there are at least twenty-five hundred Navajos in Clark County, about a quarter of the whole urban Indian population."

The life-style of the modern Native American isn't noticeably different from that of other Las Vegans, but those who treasure the culture of their ancestors are determined to preserve those traditions. You'll find their influence everywhere in Las Vegas. For a quick history lesson or more information about the first Las Vegans and their heritage, here are some sources.

Nevada State Museum and Historical Society
700 Twin Lakes Drive
Open daily, 9 A.M. to 5 P.M.
(702) 486-5205

Permanent exhibits here provide a vivid historical summary of Native American cultures in this part of the state. Ancient baskets and other artifacts are evidence of skills that existed here long before Europeans arrived.

Paiute basketmakers have been famous for their work since ancient times, when tightly woven baskets were household necessities for food gathering and cooking. When tourists and collectors started scooping them up from Las Vegas Paiutes in the 1920s, they paid a pittance for baskets that may have taken months of work. Now the baskets aren't so plentiful in shops. You're more likely to find them in museums.

Las Vegas Indian Center
2300 Bonanza Road
Las Vegas, NV 89106
(702) 647-5842

The center provides information for visitors and all sorts of services for local urban Indians from any tribe. Take a look at the Native American arts and crafts displayed in the gift shop.

Las Vegas Paiute Tribe
1 Paiute Drive
Las Vegas, NV 89106
(702) 386-3926

You'll find the entrance to the colony just off Main Street, between Washington and Owens Avenues, a few blocks west of the Old Mormon Fort. Inside the reservation at Commercial Plaza, 1225 North Main, there's a gift shop with Native American crafts for sale, including pottery, jewelry, paintings, and baskets.

Clark County Heritage Museum
1830 Boulder Highway
Henderson, NV 89015
Open daily, 9 A.M. to 4:30 P.M.
(702) 455-7955

Out of town, but on your way to Hoover Dam, you can sweep through twelve thousand years of southern Nevada history. A "Time Line" exhibit traces Native American cultures from prehistoric times to the present. Other exhibits are reminders of early railroads and mines. There's even a ghost town.

Bruno's Indian Village and Turquoise Museum
1306 Nevada Highway (U.S. 93)
Boulder City, NV 89005
(702) 293-4865

On the same route, closer to the dam, you'll find a museum and shop filled with authentic Native American lore. Two movies and a series of exhibits show you how the Ancient Ones lived in the Southwest and how modern Paiutes preserve their heritage in dance, jewelry making, and other arts. You'll also learn details about mining and polishing turquoise, and see how Paiute artists shape minerals into jewelry. A trading post and art gallery displays and sells paintings, jewelry, and souvenirs.

Moapa Tribe
1 Lincoln Drive
Moapa, NV 89025
(702) 865-2787

If you take a daytrip to the Valley of Fire, you'll pass right through the big Moapa reservation on Interstate 15, some forty miles northeast of Las Vegas. Maybe you'll stop at the small convenience store to buy a snack or cold drink. You can pick up some information about the reservation and hear about ambitious future plans.

The history of this land is dramatic. After the Civil War, President Ulysses S. Grant approved a four-thousand-acre reservation for Southern Paiutes near the

Moapa and Virgin Rivers, under the supervision of the Southeastern Nevada Indian Agency. A few years later, the reservation was cut back to a thousand acres, and Moapa Paiutes had to wait nearly a century for their original land to be restored. They finally got it back in the 1970s; and now, after years of controversy, the Moapa Tribe is free to develop the vast acres.

The Lost City Museum
721 South Moapa Valley Boulevard
Overton, NV 89040
Open daily, 8:30 A.M. to 4:30 P.M.
(702) 397-2193

This museum is on the very spot where Anasazi Indians lived in pueblos a thousand years ago. Outside the adobe museum, built in 1935, you'll see an actual pueblo foundation and an authentic reconstruction of a pit dwelling, like the ones used by the earliest residents of the Las Vegas valley. You can even climb down a ladder into the pit house. Behind the building, you'll find a collection of ancient petroglyphs (rock drawings) and nearby picnic tables.

Inside the building, there's an extensive collection of artifacts uncovered by excavations in the area. There's also a photographic record of the 1924 excavation of this site as well as other vivid historical exhibits. Overton is at the edge of the Valley of Fire State Park, some fifty miles northeast of Las Vegas, easily reached on State Route 169, via Interstate 15. For more information about the Lost City Museum, see chapter 12 page 192.

HISPANIC HERITAGE

The very name *Las Vegas* has its roots in Spain. Hispanic influence is everywhere in the city and countryside: in architecture, music, restaurant menus, and fashions. Street names and parks honor Spanish explorers. Mexican celebrations such as *Cinco de Mayo* are anticipated and recognized by the whole community as part of the city's cultural heritage.

Adventurous Mexicans came to the Southwest as early as 1540, some eighty years before the Pilgrims landed at Plymouth Rock, but the oasis with the Big Spring wasn't on their charted routes until the nineteenth century. An eighteen-year-old Spanish scout, Rafael Rivera, is given credit for discovering the meadows in 1829 while traveling with a Mexican trader, Antonio Armijo. After that, Las Vegas began to appear on maps.

In other parts of the state, Hispanic miners developed gold, silver, and copper mines. Names like Gabriel Maldonado, Don Manuel San Pedro, Jose Rodriguez, Ventura Beltran, and Francisco Pardo are sprinkled across the pages of Nevada mining history. Pioneer cattle ranchers in southern Nevada included Pedro and Bernardo Altube, who established the Spanish Ranch in 1871.

In the half century since World War II, thousands of Hispanics have migrated to the Las Vegas valley. Since 1970 the Hispanic population has grown even faster, surpassing most other ethnic groups in the community. Recent census figures show that 11.2 percent of the Clark County population has Hispanic origins. Most of these Latino Las Vegans have come from Mexico, but many arrive from Puerto Rico, Cuba, Costa Rica, Guatemala, Panama, and El Salvador. They come from South America too—from Argentina, Brazil, Colombia, Peru, and Venezuela—as well as from other parts of the United States. Through these new families, each country contributes its customs and traditions to the rich tapestry of Las Vegas culture. The tapestry changes and grows every year. To learn more about the city's Hispanic heritage, you can write or call one or more of these sources.

Nevada Association of Latin Americans
323 North Maryland Parkway
Las Vegas, NV 89101
(702) 382-6252

Latin Chamber of Commerce
829 South Sixth Street
Las Vegas, NV 89101
(702) 385-7367

***El Mundo* Newspaper**
845 North Eastern Avenue
Las Vegas, NV 89101
(702) 649-8553

La Voz de Las Vegas
1835 East Charleston Boulevard, Suite 8
Las Vegas, NV 89104
(702) 471-1192

This Spanish-language weekly circulates in Nevada, California, and Mexico. For Spanish-language television and radio, tune in to the following:

Channel 27—Las Tres Campanas TV
2887 Monja Circle
Las Vegas, NV 89104
(702) 433-0027

Channel 39—KBLR-TV
2309 Renaissance Drive
Las Vegas, NV 89119
(702) 878-9750

KDOL Radio AM-1230
740 North Valle Verde Drive
Henderson, NV 89014

AFRICAN INFLUENCES

From New Orleans jazz and Creole cooking to Moroccan menus and authentic African art, black influences turn up everywhere in the Las Vegas cultural mix. Black Americans and African immigrants make a distinctive contribution to local restaurants, art galleries, museums, shops, and entire neighborhoods.

Local historians will tell you about Jacob Dodson, a black surveyor who accompanied John C. Fremont into the Great Basin in the 1840s, but very few black settlers came to southern Nevada in the early years. More headed north and west, where gold and silver mines created jobs and attracted black business owners, ranchers, and artisans. By 1920 a few blacks lived in downtown Las Vegas, but the big migration came some twenty years later.

During World War II, workers flocked to southern Nevada to work in mines and plants supplying magnesium to the military. Most of them came from segregated states like Alabama, Mississippi, Arkansas, and Louisiana, and they were attracted to the predominantly black neighborhood across the railroad from downtown, the section now called the Westside. In those days, Las Vegas had its own prejudices. Even famous black entertainers such as Ella Fitzgerald, Pearl Bailey, and Nat "King" Cole found themselves barred from downtown hotels. But in 1955, the Moulin Rouge opened its doors on West Bonanza Avenue and became the city's first interracial hotel-casino. Big-name entertainers were brought in from all over the world, and black tourists filled the hotel. Showroom audiences were mixed when white tourists also came to see the headliners. Within ten years, the Moulin Rouge had become a meeting place for community leaders, black and white, seeking an end to segregation in Las Vegas. When the hotel was declared a historic landmark in 1993, officials who had signed the final integration documents more than twenty-five years earlier recalled their celebration at the Moulin Rouge.

The Westside, between Washington Avenue and Bonanza Road, is still considered the real center of African American Las Vegas, even though there are more black residents scattered through other neighborhoods. According to recent census figures for Clark County (including Henderson, Boulder City, Mesquite, North Las Vegas, and rural county areas), at least 9.3 percent of the population has roots in Africa. And new African residents arrive every day.

They've come from Ethopia, Ghana, Kenya, and Sierra Leone. They've left South Africa, Morocco, Egypt, and the Ivory Coast to live in Las Vegas. Many are from Caribbean countries such as Jamaica, Trinidad, and Barbados—all tracing their origins to Africa. And more African Americans are moving here from other cities in the United States.

An efficient information network serves the African American community. If you have questions, here are some places where you may find answers.

The Black Business Directory
901 West Bonanza Road #4283
Las Vegas, NV 89127
(800) 425-4223, (702) 646-4223

This book provides an extensive list of community organizations, black churches, cultural tours, restaurants, businesses, and handy phone numbers. For a closer look at the Las Vegas black community, order a copy before you leave home.

Nevada Black Chamber of Commerce
12048 West Owens Avenue
Las Vegas, NV 89106
(702) 648-6222

KCEP Radio FM-88.1
330 West Washington Avenue
Las Vegas, NV 89106
(702) 648-0104

NAACP
940 West Owens Avenue
Las Vegas, NV 89106
(702) 646-1662

Las Vegas Sentinel-Voice
(African American weekly)
1201 South Eastern Avenue
Las Vegas, NV 89104
(702) 383-4030

First African Methodist Episcopal Church
2450 Revere
North Las Vegas, NV 89030
(702) 649-1774

Holy Trinity AME Church
920 South Decatur Boulevard
Las Vegas, NV 89104
(702) 877-0790

EAST MEETS WEST

When a planeload of visitors arrives in Las Vegas from Hong Kong or Tokyo, there could be a few among them who expect to find Wild West cowboys galloping on horseback through sagebrush and cactus. Maybe they're surprised to see so many people who look just like their neighbors. In hotels, restaurants, and shops, familiar faces smile back at them.

Anybody from an Asian or Pacific Island culture is likely to find somebody from home living in Las Vegas. The city's diverse Asian community includes people from India, Thailand, Vietnam, Cambodia, Laos, and Korea, as well as China and Japan. You'll meet people from Hawaii, Samoa, Tonga, and Guam, and perhaps more immigrants from the Philippines than from any other area of the Pacific.

Asian immigration to Nevada began in the 1800s with the Chinese who worked on the railroads. Chinese doctors brought with them ancient secrets of healing that saved lives under harsh frontier conditions. Other Chinese came to work in the mines and on ranches and farms. By 1870 more than 7 percent of Nevadans were Chinese.

Japanese immigrants to Nevada were scarce in those early years, but Las Vegans who know their local history will tell you about Yonema Tomiyasu, a Japanese American farmer who provided most of the vegetables for the workers who swarmed into the Las Vegas valley during the 1930s to build the Boulder Dam. Even so, Japanese families were few in the area until the late 1980s. Then someone evidently passed the word that Las Vegas was a city of opportunity. Now Japanese businesspeople, artists, teachers, and technicians are arriving in greater numbers.

Filipinos have migrated to Nevada since the first half of the twentieth century and have settled in as permanent residents. By 1970 other Pacific Islanders began to discover Las Vegas as a place to live and work. They kept coming, followed by Vietnamese, Laotions, and East Indians. Now the city scene is brightened by this diverse mixture of lifestyles and languages. All over town, you find Asian and Pacific Island influences.

On the Las Vegas Strip, a volcano erupting outside the Mirage and a luau at the Imperial Palace may remind you of Hawaii. Asian restaurants are as diverse as the people, and several Asian markets around town provide ingredients for authentic recipes. In the new Chinatown Plaza on Spring Mountain Road, eight restaurants serve Oriental specialties, such as Cantonese dim sum, Japanese sushi, Vietnamese noodles, and Korean barbecue. The anchor store is a big supermarket stocked with Asian delicacies.

There's also an Asian Commerical Center near Maryland Parkway, between Sahara and Karen Avenues, and another Asian market downtown on Stewart Avenue. Several local publications and organizations can give you more information about Asian and Island ethnic groups.

Las Vegas Asian Times *(monthly)*
1111 Las Vegas Boulevard South
Las Vegas, NV 89104
(702) 384-1231

CityGuide U.S.A.
(monthly Japanese travel guide)
535 East St. Louis Avenue
Las Vegas, NV 89104-2563
(702) 733-2880

Philippine-American Journal *(monthly)*
3140 Polaris Avenue, Suite 7
Las Vegas, NV 89102-8361
(702) 251-9328

Asian Chamber of Commerce
4970 Arville Street, Suite 108
Las Vegas, NV 89118
(702) 367-4810

Japanese American Club of Las Vegas
1316 South Eighth Street
Las Vegas, NV 89104
(702) 382-4443

Filipino American Federation of Nevada
1111 Las Vegas Boulevard South, Suite 320
Las Vegas, NV 89104
(702) 383-6933

Thailand Nevada Association
3995 South Industrial Road
Las Vegas, NV 89103
(702) 735-0005

Las Vegas Korean Association
3855 South Valley View Boulevard, Suite 3
Las Vegas, NV 89103
(702) 252-4750

RESTAURANTS

Anywhere in the world, restaurants are still a traveler's
favorite classroom for learning about different cultures. In
the Yellow Pages of the Las Vegas telephone directory,
you'll find thirty-five pages of small type, five columns
wide, listing restaurants of all kinds. The *Las Vegas Official Visitors Guide,* published by the Convention & Visitors Authority, counts more than thirty countries
represented by restaurants in the city. Right now, here are

a few ethnic restaurants so you can start your culinary trip around the world. Hours change from season to season, so it's best to phone ahead.

African American

N'Orleans *(Southern / Creole)*
4725 Spring Mountain Road
(702) 364-8863

Sadie's Southern Dining
505 East Twain Avenue
(702) 796-4177

Chez Place *(Southern / Creole)*
910 North Martin Luther King Boulevard
(702) 648-8411

Red Sea African Restaurant
In the Sahara Paradise Plaza, facing the Sahara Hotel
2226 Paradise Road
(702) 893-1740

Gates Bar-B-Que
2710 East Desert Inn Road
(702) 369-8010

Asian

Nippon *(Japanese)*
101 Convention Center Drive
(702) 735-5565

Saigon *(Vietnamese)*
4151 West Sahara Avenue
(702) 362-9978

Kabocha *(Filipino)*
4503 Paradise Road
(702) 731-1003

Island Style *(Hawaiian)*
3909 West Sahara Avenue
(702) 871-1911

Seoul Korean Bar-B-Que
953 East Sahara Avenue
(702) 369-4123

Ghandi *(Indian)*
4080 Paradise Road at Flamingo Road
(702) 734-0094

French

Andre's
401 South Sixth Street
(702) 385-5016

Pamplemousse
400 East Sahara Avenue
(702) 733-2066

Hispanic

La Casa Cuba
2501 East Tropicana Avenue
(702) 454-6310

Dona Maria
910 Las Vegas Boulevard South
(702) 382-6538

Garcia's Mexican Restaurant
1030 East Flamingo Road
(702) 731-0628

Salvadorena
720 North Main Street
(702) 385-3600

Yoli's Brazilian Steakhouse & Seafood
3900 Paradise Road
(702) 794-0700

Italian

Battista's Hole in the Wall
4041 Audrie Street
(702) 732-1424

Cafe Milano
3900 Paradise Road, Suite X
(702) 732-2777

Middle Eastern

The Sheik
3050 East Desert Inn Road
(702) 737-1420

Moroccan

Mamounia
4632 South Maryland Parkway
(702) 597-0092

Marrakech Restaurant
3900 Paradise Road
(702) 736-7655

Chapter 9

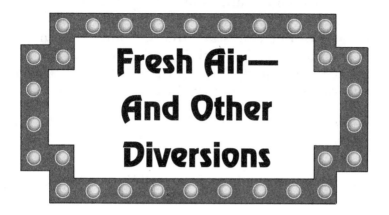

Fresh Air—
And Other
Diversions

Las Vegas is famous for indoor fun, but a city that boasts at least three hundred sunny days a year is bound to offer outdoor recreation too. When you and the kids long for fresh air, you'll find plenty to do. How about a bike ride? A game of tennis? Maybe one parent would like to do some solitary jogging or play a few rounds of golf. Or perhaps the whole family wants to swim or explore one of those entertainment parks with bumper boats and miniature racing cars. All these activities and more are possible in the city . . . sometimes right on the Strip.

The season will influence some of your choices. July and August temperatures are often too hot for vigorous exercise in the middle of the day, but early mornings are usually fresh and pleasant. In winter you can enjoy a morning swim in the city and an afternoon romp in the snow on Mt. Charleston—all in the same day. And the year around, there are outdoor "family fun" centers and shady parks for picnics. Even indoors you can bowl, iceskate, roller skate, or tone your muscles in a vigorous game of racquetball. Some visitors never realize how many different things there are to do on a Las Vegas vacation. You can start finding out, right now; a telephone call to the **Clark County Parks and Recreation Department**, (702) 455-8200, will help you find safe bicycle paths, picnic spots, maps, and special events.

BICYCLING

Bicycles for the family can be rented by the hour, day, or week. Ask at your hotel, or phone one of these bike shops in the city:

Bikes USA
1539 North Eastern Avenue
(702) 642-2453

Bike Trail
6810 West Cheyenne Avenue
(702) 656-2026

McGhies Ski Chalet
4503 West Sahara Avenue
(702) 252-8077

3310 East Flamingo Road
(702) 443-1120

Mountain bikes are a specialty at McGhies. As you might guess from the name, they also rent ski equipment in season. (See chapter 10 for skiing opportunities.) Or, if you're going to Red Rock Canyon, call ahead to pick up a bike in the little town of Blue Diamond:

Blue Diamond Bicycles
14 Cottonwood Drive
(702) 875-4500

Bicycle experts will lead the way and save you time and trouble if you sign up for a pedaling tour. To find out more, call a bike guru at one of the following places.

Downhill Bicycle Tours, Inc.
1209 South Casino Center Boulevard, Suite 122
(702) 897-8287

Escape the City Streets
P.O. Box 50262, Henderson, NV 89016
(702) 596-2953

Guides, snacks, and T-shirts are included in the price of their daily tours. If you're heading out on your own, they'll deliver bikes to your hotel and provide maps and equipment.

The Sierra Club of Las Vegas sometimes schedules bike tours in neighboring wilderness areas. Call (702) 363-3267 to find out what's happening during your visit.

GOLFING

Dedicated golfers don't have to be told that Las Vegas is Golf Heaven. Year after year, they've watched television broadcasts of championship tournaments played in the city. Whether you're a competitive golfer looking for a demanding challenge, or a casual golfer who just likes to walk around in the sunshine, you're likely to find a course in Las Vegas to suit your mood.

The city has several private golf clubs, but all courses listed here are open to the public. Most of these are eighteen-hole courses, but we found one with nine holes. All have snack bars and/or restaurants and all have golf equipment for rent. Some offer professional lessons by appointment. Green fees vary widely—from as low as $5 for nine holes up to $150 for eighteen—so it's wise to do a little telephone research ahead of time. You'll have to phone for tee times anyway.

Angel Park Golf Club
100 South Rampart Boulevard
(702) 254-4653; for restaurant and lounge
reservations, call: (702) 254-3250

Angel Park has two eighteen-hole Arnold Palmer courses, both par 71. The Palm course is 5,634 yards, and the Mountain course is 5,751 yards. You'll find a lighted driving range, golf shop, snack bar, and locker rooms. Mandatory golf carts are included in the fee.

Boulder City Golf Course
500 Greenway Road, Boulder City
(702) 293-9236

Outside Las Vegas and closer to Lake Mead (just south of U.S. Highway 93), this course has reasonable rates—eighteen holes and a par 72 for 6,132 yards. You can rent your clubs in the golf shop and relax in the clubhouse restaurant, coffee shop, or snack bar.

Craig Ranch Golf Club
628 West Craig Road (three miles north, off I-15)
(702) 642-9700

In a rural setting, you'll find eighteen holes, par 70. It's a 6,001-yard course, and there's a driving range, golf carts, clubhouse, pro shop, and snack bar. Ads promise "six thousand trees." Rates are among the lowest.

Desert Rose Golf Course
5483 Clubhouse Drive (off Sahara Avenue)
(702) 431-4653

This Clark County public facility offers all the amenities of a private club at very reasonable rates. You can rent golf equipment for the day, and professional instruction is available. There's a driving range and eighteen holes, par 71 for the 6,135-yard course. Enjoy the restaurant, coffee shop, or cocktail lounge. Reservations are suggested.

Las Vegas Golf Club
4349 Vegas Drive (off U.S. 95, near Decatur
Boulevard and Washington Avenue)
(702) 646-3003

Under the same management as Desert Rose, this eighteen-hole course, par 72, has even lower fees. Same list of facilities, including electric carts, rental equipment, restaurant, and pro shop. Call for reservations.

The Legacy Golf Club
130 Par Excellence Drive, Henderson
(702) 897-2187; club restaurant: (702) 897-2108

Outside the city in suburban Henderson, the Legacy is easy to reach from the Strip, via Sunset Road and Green Valley Parkway. Tournament fans know the Legacy as the Las Vegas course where qualifying competitions have been held, several years in a row, for the U.S. Open. Designed by Arthur Hills, this is an eighteen-hole course, 6,211 yards, par 72. The resort is a favorite spot among Las Vegans for weddings and other celebrations. Call for information and don't be surprised if rates are high.

Los Prados Golf & Country Club
5150 Los Prados Circle (take U.S. 95 to Lone
Mountain Road)
(702) 645-5696

Located in a planned residential community, this public course has eighteen holes, par 70 for 5,348 yards. The clubhouse has the usual comforts, including locker rooms, pro shop, and restaurant. Rates are surprisingly modest. Make reservations.

North Las Vegas City Golf Course
324 East Brooks Avenue
(702) 649-7171

Just for fun, you can rent some clubs and play nine holes on this 1,128-yard course, par 27. At night the course is lighted. Unless rates have changed in recent months, they're so low you won't believe them.

Painted Desert Golf Course
5555 Painted Mirage Road (northwest on U.S. 95
to Ann Road)
(702) 645-2568

The setting is scenic and rates are moderately high at this eighteen-hole course, 6,323 yards, par 72. Phone for details.

Royal Kenfield Country Club
1 Showboat Country Club Drive, Henderson
(702) 434-7058

Serious golfers often sign up for lessons at this demanding eighteen-hole, 7,023-yard, par 72 course. Practice facilities and a lush setting are prime attractions. Rates are high, but lower than those at the top, and a mandatory golf cart is included. There's no big restaurant on the site, but you'll find a snack bar and beverage cart. The Legacy resort is close by. Phone ahead to rent clubs and reserve green times.

Sahara Country Club
1911 East Desert Inn Road
(702) 796-0016

This course has everything you'd expect in a Las Vegas golf club, including the lighted driving range, clubhouse, restaurants, power carts, and all the usual amenities. It's an eighteen-hole course, 6,418 yards, par 71. Rates are near the top, but include a mandatory golf cart.

Sheraton Desert Inn Country Club
3145 Las Vegas Boulevard South
(702) 733-4290; hotel: (702) 733-4444

Right on the Strip, the famous Desert Inn course reopened late in 1994 after months of renovations, ready for national tournaments scheduled in 1995. The new look includes a lake system covering six acres, a continuous eight-foot-wide cart path, eighteen new greens, eighty-seven new or remodeled bunkers, and eighteen new individual tee monuments. Rates are the most expensive in Las Vegas, but package plans are available if you stay at the Sheraton Desert Inn resort. Ask your travel agent or call the hotel.

Palm Valley Golf Club
9201 Del Webb Boulevard
Pro shop: (702) 363-4373; restaurant: (702) 363-5330

Highland Falls Golf Club
10201 Sun City Boulevard
Pro shop: (702) 254-7010; restaurant: (702) 254-0767

These are the two eighteen-hole courses at the Golf Clubs of **Sun City Las Vegas**. Each has its own pro shop and restaurant.

And There's More . . .

Golf courses seem to spring up overnight in the Las Vegas area. One of the newest, with views of Mt.

Charleston and Sheep Mountain, opened recently on the Southern Paiute reservation north of Las Vegas on U.S. Highway 95. The 7,189-yard course (par 72) is called Nu-Wav Kaiv in Paiute, meaning "Snow Mountain." This is the first of four courses in the works for the reservation, along with a clubhouse, casino, hotels, and a theme park. Snow Mountain golf course is part of the first phase of an 810-acre master-planned residential community.

MINIATURE GOLF
AND RACING CARS

Most kids love to hit a ball around a miniature golf course. Sometimes they're more skillful than Mom and Dad! For a spur-of-the-moment game any day of the week, take them to one of the following "family fun" parks.

Formula K Family Fun Park
2980 South Sandhill Road
(702) 431-7223

This park focuses on miniature golf, go-carts, and games. Golfers of any size can play thirty-six holes. Those under 54 inches tall can steer small racing cars around a miniature track. There's also a large go-cart track for bigger racers as well as a game room. Phone for reservations.

Scandia Family Fun Center
2900 Sirius Avenue (west of the Strip and I-15, between Sahara Avenue and Spring Mountain Road)
Open daily, 10 A.M. to midnight
(702) 364-0070

Not just one, but *three* eighteen-hole mini–golf courses invite you to meander around the landscaped grounds.

There's also a downsized racetrack with miniature racing cars, baseball batting cages, bumper boats, and a big video arcade. Hours may change with the season, so call ahead.

Funtazmic
4975 Polaris Avenue
Open Monday–Thursday, 4 to 10 P.M.; Friday, 4 P.M. to midnight; Saturday, 10 A.M to midnight; Sunday, 10 A.M. to 10 P.M.
(702) 795-4386

This park skips the golf and concentrates on thrills and speed. Custom-built race cars zoom around a double figure-eight raceway, and bumper boats test your steering skills. Anyone shorter than 54 inches will find scaled-down fun in Li'l World, where everything is designed for kids. A game of Battle Quest puts you in the middle of a shooting war. Indoor video games exercise your elbows. Weather may affect outdoor hours. Call ahead.

TENNIS AND RACQUETBALL

If tennis is your game, you may have chosen a hotel with built-in courts. For a small fee, some of the big resorts open their courts to players who aren't hotel guests. Racquetball enthusiasts can buy a guest pass to play at local athletic clubs. Reservations are required at some of these courts (a good idea at most of them), but there are several walk-in-anytime public tennis courts where you can play for nothing. Here's a list of possibilities.

Hotels and Resorts

Aladdin Hotel
3667 Las Vegas Boulevard South
Call for reservations: (702) 736-0111 or (800) 634-3424

The Aladdin has three outdoor racquetball courts, two of them lighted. There are three outdoor tennis courts and a morning clinic with a tennis pro.

Alexis Park Resort Hotel
375 East Harmon Avenue
(702) 796-3300 or (800) 582-2228

The Alexis Park Resort has two lighted outdoor courts. Hotel guests have first choice, but you can ask.

Bally's Las Vegas
3645 Las Vegas Boulevard South
(702) 739-4598, (800) 634-3434

Bally's has a huge spread of ten outdoor courts, five of them lighted. Reservations are necessary between 8 A.M. and 8 P.M.

Caesars Palace
3570 Las Vegas Boulevard South
(702) 731-7786, (800) 634-6001

Caesars has five outdoor courts, where visitors can play in splendid surroundings for an hourly fee. The racquetball courts are located in the men's and women's spas.

Flamingo Hilton
3555 Las Vegas Boulevard South
(702) 733-3344

When hotel guests aren't using all of them, you can play on one of the four lighted outdoor courts, for a fee.

Sheraton Desert Inn
3145 Las Vegas Boulevard South
Call for reservations: (702) 733-4577

The Sheraton Desert Inn offers visitors a daily pass at a moderate fee. You'll find ten outdoor courts, five of which are lighted. Between matches, you can test the jogging track.

The Union Plaza Hotel
1 Main Street
(702) 386-2110

This hotel in downtown Las Vegas has four lighted outdoor courts and a jogging track. Hotel guests have first pick.

Away from the Hotels

University of Nevada at Las Vegas
near Harmon Avenue at Swenson Street
(702) 895-3150

This on-campus facility has twelve outdoor tennis courts and eight indoor racquetball courts, where you can play for a tiny guest fee. Reservations are advised.

The Las Vegas Athletic Club
Eastside: 1070 Sahara Avenue
(702) 733-1919

Westside: 3315 Spring Mountain Road
(702) 362-3720

Racquetball courts are available at both club sites. Each has eight courts open to visitors who have guest passes, usually $10 each. In an all-night town, you won't be surprised to learn that Club East is open 24 hours. Call for reservations.

Las Vegas Sporting House
3025 Industrial Road (behind the Mirage and Treasure Island)
Call for information and reservations: (702) 733-8999

Here you'll find ten racqetball courts, two lighted outdoor tennis courts, and two squash courts. The all-day fee usually is $20, but you'll be given a discount if you're staying at one of the hotels.

Sunset Park
2575 East Sunset Drive
Call for reservations: (702) 455-8200

This public park has eight lighted outdoor tennis courts, popular enough to make reservations necessary. (No reservations are needed for tossing frisbees on the green.)

No-Fee Public Parks and Schools

Other parks have free tennis courts. If your timing is right, you'll find an empty court, and there are no fees. The rec center has three outdoor courts, lighted at night. At the public parks listed, you'll find two lighted outdoor courts.

East Las Vegas Park & Recreation Center
5700 East Missouri Avenue

Laurelwood Park
4300 Newcastle Road

Paradise Park Recreation Center
4770 South Harrison Drive

Paul Meyer Park
4525 New Forest Drive

Winterwood Park
5310 Consul Avenue

Visitors are allowed to use tennis courts at the following public schools. Wait until after 5 P.M. when school is in session, but play anytime during weekends and vacations.

Cannon Junior High School
5850 Euclid Avenue

Three outdoor courts, not lighted.

Orr Junior High School
1562 East Katie Avenue

Four outdoor courts, not lighted.

Woodbury Junior High School
3875 East Harmon Avenue

Three courts, not lighted, Monday through Friday.

BOWLING

Who bowls at 3 A.M.? Obviously, some bowlers prefer hours that seem strange to the rest of us. Otherwise, why would Las Vegas bowling centers stay open around-the-clock? All four of the following never close.

Gold Coast Hotel & Casino
4000 West Flamingo Road

(702) 367-4700

Choose one of 72 lanes.

Showboat
2800 Fremont Street

(702) 385-9153

Serves even more bowlers with 106 lanes.

Sam's Town Bowling Center
5111 Boulder Highway

(702) 454-8022

Keeps the balls rolling down 56 lanes.

Santa Fe Lanes
4949 North Rancho Drive
(702) 658-4995
Stays open round-the-clock with 60 lanes.

SKATING ON ICE OR WHEELS

Ice-skating

When the temperature outdoors climbs toward a hundred, you can cool off inside the professional ice arena:

Santa Fe Hotel
4949 North Rancho Drive
(702) 658-4900
Phone ahead for information about lessons, skate rentals, hours, and admission prices.

Roller Skating

Las Vegas has roller-skating rinks at three locations. A fourth is in suburban Henderson.

Crystal Palace Skating Centers
4680 Boulder Highway
(702) 458-7107
4740 South Decatur Boulevard
(702) 253-9832
3901 North Rancho Drive
(702) 645-4892

Playland
1110 Lake Mead Drive, Henderson
(702) 564-2790

SWIMMING

By this time, you've discovered the swimming pool at your hotel or motel and you know about **Wet 'n' Wild** on the Strip (see chapter 5, page 68). Pools are almost everywhere you look in Las Vegas. Several public parks have pools open from June to Labor Day. For more information about these and other public recreation possibilities, call the **Clark County Parks and Recreation Department**, (702) 455-8200.

HORSEBACK RIDING

Horses, always major players in our Wild West fantasies, are part of the Las Vegas vacation picture—and not just for horse-race gamblers. Dude ranches are no longer the celebrity-filled resorts they were a half century ago, but riding stables and trail rides are still popular with visitors.

Bonnie Springs Old Nevada Village
1 Gunfighter Lane (off SR-159)
Open daily
Call to reserve your horses: (702) 875-4191

Desert trails west of Las Vegas are within easy reach of these stables, which are next to an amusement park, where you and the kids can explore a reconstructed old western town and witness staged adventures. For more information about Bonnie Springs, see chapter 10, page 156.

Mountain T. Ranch
140 Kyle Canyon Road
Call for schedules and reservations: (702) 656-8025

Ideal for guided trail rides in the high desert near Mt. Charleston, this ranch is relatively new in this area, open since February 1994, but the family who runs it has been "in the horse business" for thirty years, offering trail rides in other states, including Florida.

LET'S TAKE A WALK

All you need is a map, comfortable shoes, and a sense of direction. Explore Las Vegas neighborhoods at random on your own, or sign up for a walking tour with someone who knows the area. Call to find out what you can see and do. Brochures promise nature walks, Native American lore, and no more than two miles on foot, round trip.

Discover Tours
4255 West Viking Road, #648
(702) 873-6962

PROTECTED WILDERNESS AREAS

As the city expands, some of the surrounding desert inevitably disappears, but many Las Vegans are determined to preserve parts of the wilderness. **Las Vegas Wash**, a natural wetlands area northeast of the city, is fed by Las Vegas wastewater and runoff. The marshes attract more than 260 species of birds and other wildlife. Soon it will become the **Clark County Wetland Park** with a visitor center, marked hiking trails, and a series of fifteen damlike structures to control erosion and create ponds. A consortium of three companies is investing $14.5 million to develop a master plan for the park. Next time you come to Las Vegas, it may be ready to explore.

An older park near the city is already a favorite outdoor destination for visitors, especially those interested in desert geology and history. **Floyd Lamb State Park**, about twelve miles north of Las Vegas off U.S. Highway 95, has shady hiking trails, hot springs, picnic tables and grills, and four small lakes stocked with rainbow trout in winter, catfish in summer, and fishing is allowed.

The **Tule Springs Ranch**, now part of the 2,040-acre park, once was a thriving farm and a haven for early residents of the Las Vegas valley. Later it became a popular dude ranch, catering to visitors seeking quick Nevada divorces. While offering horseback riding, tennis, swimming, hayrides, and dances, it was still a working ranch, cultivating vegetables and livestock. Now when you take a self-guided tour of the ranch, you'll see a herd of cattle, peacocks, ducks, geese, and chickens still there. You can also visit the caretaker's house, stables, dairy barn, and an old adobe hut built in 1916 by John Herbert Nay, the first farmer on the site.

Archaeologists and geologists love the place. Beds of white mud surrounding the park are remnants of Ice Age lakes that once filled central parts of the valley. Researchers exploring these muddy spots have discovered treasures of Ice Age fossils, from small freshwater snails to the bones of mammoths. They've also uncovered remains of giant sloths, bison, and camels.

Moving On . . .

Now that we've left the glitter behind, we'll venture farther into the desert. Section 2 of this book suggests some more desert adventures within easy reach of Las Vegas.

2

Desert Adventures

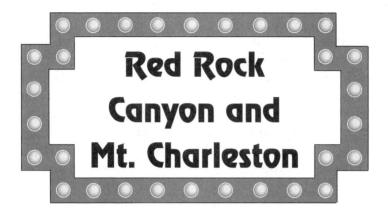

Chapter 10

Red Rock Canyon and Mt. Charleston

"Why didn't somebody tell us about this?" they ask.

First-time visitors to Red Rock Canyon, awed by the sheer size of those patchwork-colored sandstone cliffs, are astonished to find such wild natural beauty so close to Glitter City. And if they meet winter skiers heading for Mt. Charleston, they're even more astounded. *Skiing? Here?* This is southern Nevada! Who would expect to find snow just an hour away from casino swimming pools, where vacationers lounge in swimsuits?

From the window of your hotel room on the Strip, you see jagged mountains on the western horizon, a dramatic backdrop for the city's million lights. You're looking at the Spring Mountains Range, a fifty-mile wall guarding the valley. That prominent peak, slightly to your right, is Mount Charleston, rising 11,918 feet above sea level. It's only thirty-five miles from the city, in the Toiyabe National Forest . . . close enough for a daytrip.

Those lower peaks to the left of Charleston will help you locate Red Rock Canyon, even closer to the city. This natural "Jurassic Park" in the Mohave Desert is a wilderness where lizards and tortoises live among wild burros and jackrabbits. In less than an hour, you and your family could be in a world that was once the province of dinosaurs.

You can *sample* both places in one day, but don't be surprised if you find yourself wishing for more time to explore. After a preliminary visit, you may want to return later for several days of camping, hiking, or winter skiing. To make the most of a one-day excursion—from city to desert to mountains—sit down with a good map and do a little advance planning. How much time do you want to allow for driving and walking? Would you rather have a picnic lunch in the canyon or table service in the dining room of a mountain resort? What kind of weather can you expect?

Summer afternoons in Red Rock Canyon can be blazing hot, 110° F or so, while the mountain top is a cool 70°. In winter you may need to wear long johns on the mountain while rock climbers in the canyon are comfortable in light jackets. Let the season and your itinerary dictate what you'll wear and what emergency supplies you'll take. There's more than one way to sample the natural wonders of desert and forest . . . and more than a few tempting stops and side excursions.

From the Strip, take Interstate 15 to Charleston Boulevard (which becomes State Route 159) and head west into Red Rock Canyon. You can get there in half an hour, spend the morning exploring the scenic loop, and then move on to Mount Charleston for the afternoon.

RED ROCK CANYON NATIONAL CONSERVATION AREA

The first thing you'll notice is the variety of colors. Those hills and rocks are not just red—some cliffs and peaks look pink, orange, or yellow with purple shadows. No wonder they're called Calico Hills. Higher mountains in the distance seem to be striped, with layers of gray on top of red. Patches of cactus and Joshua trees beside the road remind you that you're in the Mohave Desert, the same desert containing Death Valley National Monument.

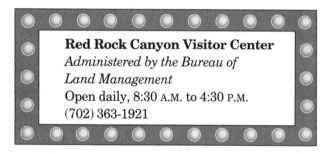

Red Rock Canyon Visitor Center
Administered by the Bureau of
Land Management
Open daily, 8:30 A.M. to 4:30 P.M.
(702) 363-1921

Young naturalists will be full of questions. So will their parents. "Why is the rock red?" If you make the Visitor Center your first stop, you'll find answers to those questions and more.

This rocky wilderness covers more than 195,000 acres, so you'll need to pinpoint an area to explore. More than half of these acres are a very recent addition. On Nevada's 130th birthday, October 31, 1994, President Clinton signed into law a bill adding 112,000 acres to the previously designated 83,000 acres of the Red Rock Canyon National Conservation Area. Both houses of Congress had voted to double the size of the protected federal land. Now the Red Rock area, managed by the Las Vegas District of the Bureau of Land Management (BLM), extends northward almost to Mt. Charleston, to the edge of the Toiyabe National Forest.

Soon after you enter the BLM land on State Route 159, you'll see the Visitor Center, just past the Red Spring Picnic Area. There's a short nature trail outside the building, with detailed markers introducing you to desert plants. Inside you'll find excellent exhibits tracing the geological history of the land, showing how it might have looked hundreds of millions of years ago. Illustrated charts show you what kind of animals and plants existed at various stages of evolution, from primitive sea creatures to present-day lizards and coyotes. One exhibit explains the red color of rocks—iron deposits. After spending a little time with these exhibits, you'll know what to look for outside.

Be sure to pick up some maps and brochures to help you decide what to see and where to go in the limited time you have. Children can ask for a *Junior Ranger Discovery Book,* full of intriguing drawings and information about animals, plants, and rocks in Red Rock Canyon. They'll learn how to recognize animal tracks and different kinds of cacti. Before long they'll be looking for coyote paw prints or lizard tracks in the sand and telling you exactly where to watch for wild burros and bighorn sheep. Later each child can earn a Junior Ranger badge by answering questions in the discovery book and submitting it to a Red Rock ranger.

Children and adults who live in Las Vegas—or visitors who have enough time—can join some of the organized free activities at Red Rock Canyon. During the school year, rangers plan old-fashioned sing-alongs for all ages and lead hikes and climbing expeditions to specific areas of the park. Some are as short as one mile, such as the walk to **Lost Creek,** where you learn how Native Americans lived in the old days. Others are classified as "very strenuous," like the eleven-mile **Ascent**

to Bridge Mountain, for a view of the whole valley. Reservations are necessary for these hikes, but you can find out about them ahead of time, before leaving home, by calling the Visitor Center or by writing:

United States Department of the Interior
Bureau of Land Management
Red Rock Canyon National Conservation Area
4765 Vegas Drive
P.O. Box 26569
Las Vegas, NV 89126

A conversation with one of the helpful rangers can send you and your family off in the right direction for your own self-guided expedition. For a morning-only tour, they'll recommend the clearly marked thirteen-mile **Scenic Drive**, a one-way road where bicycles are allowed. The loop starts near the Visitor Center and returns to SR-159 about two miles south. The road opens at 8 A.M., and you can make the trip in less than half an hour or spend the whole morning exploring. You may be tempted to spend the whole day. (In his *Nevada Handbook,* travel writer Deke Castleman is even more enthusiastic: "You could then spend another six days hiking around the . . . park, or devote a lifetime to climbing the 1,500 known routes up the red rock.")

The Scenic Drive is flexible enough to allow you to get out of the car at designated parking areas and hike down one of the many trails. At the first two pullouts, you'll find short trails leading toward the base of the **Calico Hills**. If the season is right, nature lovers can look for rain pools, where insects may be hatching. A little farther on, a dirt road leads to the **Sandstone Quarry**, where great blocks of stone were once cut for early Las Vegas buildings, long before the land was protected by conservation programs. Now the removal of rocks is strictly prohibited.

If you have time for just one stop, don't miss the **Lost Creek Children's Discovery Trail**. It's only half a mile long and it leads you through some spectacular scenery. It's also near the **Willow Spring picnic area**, a perfect place to unpack your lunch (unless you're planning a later meal at Mt. Charleston). Charcoal grills are provided for outdoor cooks. From here you can walk into **Lost Creek Canyon** to find a year-round spring, but don't drink the water.

If the weather is hot, you can cool off in **Ice Box Canyon**, the next stop along the way, where steep walls protect trails from the blazing sun. You may even see a small waterfall, if there has been any recent rain. Last stop on the loop is the **Pine Creek Canyon** overlook and a short trail leading to the ruins of an old homestead. An unexpected grove of ponderosa pines grows along a creek in the canyon. Your Junior Rangers will tell you these trees are usually found at much higher elevations, above six thousand feet.

Whatever you do, make sure to have plenty of film in the camera. Red Rock Canyon is one of the most photographed spots in Nevada. More than a million visitors pour in every year, sometimes crowding the Scenic Drive with cars. Now the BLM is talking about limiting the number of vehicles to 275 at a time. Eventually, it hopes to run shuttle buses from the Visitor Center to reduce the traffic.

Budding geologists will be fascinated by those mysteriously striped cliffs and mountains seen from the road. Professional geologists are even more interested. The gray layers of rock on top are hundreds of millions of years older than the red layers underneath, breaking the fundamental rule of "superposition" taught in geology classes: *Old rocks always underlie younger rocks.* But not always. In his illustrated *Geology of the Great Basin,* Nevada geologist Bill Fiero describes Red Rock Canyon as an exception to the rule. "The old gray Paleozoic limestones are thrust over the younger red rocks of the Jurassic. . . . The breaking of the rule is so flagrantly and beautifully illustrated by the sharp color contrast that many introductory geology textbooks have a photograph of this feature."

The feature is called the **Keystone Thrust Fault**, a phenomenon that attracts geologists to Red Rock Canyon from around the world. To their trained eyes, the layering seems impossible. How did these ancient gray limestones, at least 270 million years old, come to be on top of red sandstone that didn't exist until maybe 180 million years ago? The only explanation, scientists say, is a sudden upheaval, a cracking and shifting of the earth's crust, about 65 million years ago. Separate plates of this crust collided with such force that layers of rock were tilted up (see those vertical layers?), and old rocks under the surface were thrown up and over the younger Jurassic sandstone. Some scientists believe that the timing of this prehistoric upheaval may hold a clue to the disappearance of the dinosaurs.

At the end of the Scenic Drive, you have to decide which way to turn. If you're going to combine desert and mountains in a one-day trip, you'll turn left on State Route 159 and go back past the Visitor Center toward Las Vegas, looking for the turnoff to Mt. Charleston. What happens if you turn right? For one thing, it will mean postponing Mt. Charleston until another day. Here are a few alternatives.

**Spring Mountain Ranch
State Park**
Red Rock Canyon National
Conservation Area
Ranch House/Visitor Center
Open Friday–Monday (and on
  holidays), 10 A.M. to 4 P.M.
Park open daily, 8 A.M. to dusk
(702) 875-4141

See how pioneers lived in the 1860s, watch for birds and burros in a wildlife habitat, stroll across green lawns, and glimpse a rural hideaway for a 1950s billionaire. If your timing is right, you may join the audience for a concert or community theater production on the outdoor stage. In summer, staff members and volunteers wear pioneer costumes and demonstrate the skills and crafts of early ranchers. This **Living History program** is especially popular with schoolchildren and their parents.

Soon after you turn right on SR-159, you'll see the ranch up ahead in the shelter of the **Wilson Cliffs**. Named for the Wilson family who owned the ranch for three generations, 1876 to 1948, these steep sandstone cliffs were a landmark for early travelers through the Las Vegas valley. They still guide modern motorists to the 528-acre Spring Mountains Ranch, a state park since 1974. Now within the Red Rock Canyon National Conservation Area, the ranch is managed by the Nevada State Parks Division.

From the road, it looks like a prosperous working ranch with neat white fences and a rambling red-and-white house shaded by big oak trees. Drive up to the

parking lot and you'll find picnic tables, drinking fountains, and indoor restrooms. At the Visitor Center, inside
the immaculately maintained ranch house, you can pick
up maps of the park and take a free tour of the house
once owned by tycoon Howard Hughes. All the rooms
are still furnished as they were in the 1950s. Built in the
late 1940s for *Lum and Abner* radio star Chet Lauck,
the house later changed hands several times. It was sold
to actress Vera Krupp of the German munitions family,
among others, and later to billionaire Hughes before it
became a state park.

The original sandstone-block farmhouse still stands
on the property near a reconstructed blacksmith shop,
where old bellows and tools look as if they've been in use
for a century. Ask about guided tours to **Lake Harriet**,
a reservoir in the foothills above the ranch, and you'll
see why the pastures are so green. Abundant water for
the ranch comes from this reservoir, fed year-round by
Sandstone Spring. The surrounding wetlands attract
all sorts of wildlife, including birds, snakes, lizards, and
bighorn sheep.

Back at the entrance, notice the outdoor stage on the
south side of the driveway. This is a permanent structure, used by local theater groups and other performers,
financed by donations to the State Parks Cultural
Board. Audiences bring their own blankets or lawn
chairs and sometimes assemble early for picnics on
the spot. Tickets for the summer productions must be
reserved ahead of time. For information about current
programs, call (702) 875-4141.

Overnight camping isn't permitted here, or anywhere
else in the Red Rock Canyon National Conservation
Area. There's no lodging in the park, but you will find a
comfortable, child-friendly motel next to a small western
theme park, just half a mile down the road.

**Bonnie Springs Ranch
and Old Nevada Village**
1 Gunfighter Lane (off State Route 159)
Open daily, 10:30 A.M. to 6 P.M.
(702) 875-4191

The original Bonnie Springs was a watering hole used by pioneer wagon trains on their way to California. Now, on the site of an old cattle ranch built in 1843, the modern Bonnie Springs is a motel with fifty guest rooms, a swimming pool, and a restaurant with simple meals at moderate prices.

For children the big attraction here is **Old Nevada Village**, a little amusement park where an old western town has been reconstructed. Performers stage Wild West melodramas and mock gunfights on the main street, and visitors explore rows of weathered buildings housing the saloon, ice-cream parlor, opera house, sheriff's office, and country stores. On the edge of town, there's a train to take you on a short ride. Bonnie Springs Ranch also has riding stables, a duck pond, and a petting zoo.

From here it's easy to find your way back to Las Vegas. State Route 159 joins Highway 160 at a settlement called Blue Diamond. Go east on 160 until you reach northbound Interstate 15. That takes you right back to the Strip.

PREVIEW OF MT. CHARLESTON

What if you had turned left instead of right on State Route 159 this morning when you completed the Scenic

Drive in Red Rock Canyon? Suppose you had chosen to stay with your original plan to include Mt. Charleston in the day's excursion. To reach the mountain from the canyon, turn left from the Scenic Drive road and retrace your route on SR-159, back into the city, until you reach Rainbow Boulevard. Turn left again and pick up U.S. Highway 95. If you need reassurance that you're heading in the right direction, look for signs pointing toward Tonopah and Reno, and you're on your way.

At Kyle Canyon Road (SR-157) turn left into the **Toiyabe National Forest**. This is just one segment of a huge forest preserve that covers 3,861,166 acres, scattered in patches through Nevada and eastern California mountains.

As the road winds and climbs steeply into the forest, the landscape changes dramatically. A few miles back, you were driving through bare desert, past an occasional Joshua tree or a few sprigs of mesquite. Now you're surrounded by shady junipers and pines.

The **Mount Charleston National Recreation Area**, managed by the Las Vegas Ranger District of the United States Department of Agriculture Forestry Service, is a favorite getaway spot for Las Vegans. It's a great place for summer camping, hiking, horseback riding, and backpacking at high altitudes, 6,000 to 8,500 feet above sea level. And what could be more exotic, just an hour away from Glitter Gulch, than a winter sleigh ride or an afternoon of skiing? For some of these activities, you'll have to plan ahead, but a spur-of-the-moment drive up the mountain will give you a preview of things to do on your next visit.

Suppose it's lunchtime and you're ready for a leisurely restaurant meal with a view. You're looking for a relaxed place with hospitable rest rooms and a menu that's varied enough to please the pickiest and hungriest children and adults. On Kyle Canyon Road, you'll find two popular resort restaurants, each with its own individual appeal.

Mt. Charleston Hotel
2 Kyle Canyon Road
(702) 872-5500, (800) 794-3456

The minute you walk into the lobby, you'll know you want to stay awhile. If the weather is cold outside, a cozy fireplace beckons you to warm your toes. In summer the high ceiling and tree-trunk pillars make you feel immediately cooler. The dining room looks even more inviting, with wraparound windows providing a sweeping view of the garden and surrounding hills. Open rafters and mounted trophies add to the hunting-lodge atmosphere. Menu choices include salads, pasta dishes, meat and fish entrees, and yummy desserts. Prices are moderate and service is friendly.

Back in the lobby, you can ask hotel employees for information about the recreation area. They'll answer your questions, direct you to the Forest Ranger Station, and provide brochures and flyers about local events and attractions. Looking ahead to a return visit, ask about room rates and package plans.

Until very recently, the Mt. Charleston Hotel was the only lodging on the mountain. An older and very popular "lodge" up the road was strictly a place to eat, drink, and relax between hikes and sleigh rides, until it recently added a cluster of bed-and-breakfast cabins to provide for overnighters.

Mt. Charleston Resort
at the top of Kyle Canyon Road
(702) 386-6899, (702) 872-5408

Formerly called "Mt. Charleston Lodge," this restaurant/ bar/lounge has been here since the late 1950s, but now the whole place is getting a face-lift. The twenty new rustic-looking cabins are anything but rustic inside. Each cottage has its own gas-log fireplace, a whirlpool bath, and a private balcony overlooking the canyon. Two of the cabins are specially equipped to accommodate wheelchairs. As for breakfast, guests can have it delivered to the cabin or stroll over to the lodge for a sociable meal in the dining room. Either way, it's part of the bed-and-breakfast package.

At lunch and dinner, the restaurant is a favorite with entertainers and other Las Vegans who come for the food (sometimes wild game) and the spectacular view. Close to several hiking trails, the place is also a haven for campers, hikers, and cross-country skiers. The atmosphere is appropriately casual, and the parking lot is usually full, especially on weekends. Local residents gather here for community events and family celebrations. Tourists browse in the antique shop next door.

For cars, the road ends at the Mt. Charleston Resort. From there you have a choice of several hiking trails, but it's important to know exactly where you're going. If you plan to do any hiking, camping, or picnicking, be sure to stop at the **Kyle Canyon Ranger Station** on your way up the mountain. You'll find a big relief map of the area to help you find your way around and lots of information about the natural environment and history of the place.

Rangers will answer your questions and direct you to restrooms and drinking water. They'll give you a list of easy trails—and some very strenuous ones—and will provide an individual map for each trail you plan to follow. These little maps are packed with indispensible information for safe hiking and informed sight-seeing.

A typical map-brochure tells you how to find the trailhead, where to park, how much time to allow, what you'll see along the way, and which seasons are best. It also warns you about avalanche areas, dangerous turns, and steep drops. Each map includes a list of trail rules and reminders. In case you need more information, there's a number to call in Las Vegas: (702) 873-8800.

Short hikes on the ranger's list include a few that begin at the end of Kyle Canyon Road. Easiest and safest for small children is the half-mile **Little Falls Trail**, rewarding for nature lovers yet brief enough to include in your single-day, all-purpose tour. Others are more strenuous and require advance planning.

Mary Jane Falls Trail is another matter—just 1.2 miles each way, but difficult enough to take at least two hours for a round trip. If you have time, it's worth climbing from 7,840 to 8,880 feet above sea level to see the falls, especially in spring. Two caves near the bottom of the cliff are visible in summer.

Cathedral Rock Trail is a little longer and takes about an hour each way. Summer is best, when wildflowers are in bloom. Winter can be dangerous when snowslides can build into major avalanches. You can see the avalanche chute from the trail. At the top, you'll find a spectacular view of Kyle Canyon, but rangers will warn you to watch your step *and your children* at the edge of the cliff.

South Loop Trail is *not* one of the easy hikes. This trail requires careful planning, some training, and overnight camping. It's included here because it's part of the **Mount Charleston National Recreation Trail**, a major attraction for experienced backpackers and one of three national hiking trails within the sprawling Toiyabe National Forest. The steep trail leads from Cathedral Rock to the very peak of Mt. Charleston. On a clear day, rangers will tell you, the view from the peak extends more than two hundred miles in every direction. You can see Telescope Peak in Death Valley, some eighty-five miles to the northwest, and Mt. Whitney beyond that. To the east, there's Lake Mead and Arizona. Up north you spot the Nevada Test Site, where the Atomic Energy Commission detonated aboveground nuclear explosions in the 1950s.

The hike covers 8.3 miles in each direction (9 miles, according to some Forest Service publications) and climbs from 7,600 to 11,918 feet above sea level. Expert hikers say they can complete the climb in about six hours, but that doesn't count time out for rest stops, exploring, and picnicking. Most are prepared to camp overnight.

There's another trail to the peak from SR-158, the road that connects Kyle Canyon to Lee Canyon, but the **North Loop** is two miles longer and even more strenuous. Hiking time for that trail is estimated at eight hours each way.

If you plan to do any camping next time you visit Mt. Charleston, be sure to request information before leaving home. The Forest Service will send you a list of campgrounds in the area with details about facilities, fees, and reservations. They'll also send a valuable library of maps and brochures about picnic sites, hiking trails, and current conditions you should know about. Sometimes they enclose a special publication, such as their illustrated folder about the Bristlecone Pine, "nature's oldest living thing." The address is:

U.S.D.A. Forest Service
Toiyabe National Forest
Spring Mountains National Recreation Area
2881 South Valley View Boulevard #16
Las Vegas, NV 89102
(702) 873-8800

Full-service camping in the **Spring Mountains National Recreation Area**, including Mt. Charleston, is available from May 1 through September 30, seven days a week. Reservations must be made at least three days in advance, but you can make them up to 120 days ahead of time. For twenty-four-hour information, call (702) 222-1597; for reservations, (800) 280-2267.

WINTER WONDERLAND

If your family enjoys winter sports and if you're planning a winter trip, you'll need another whole set of directions. Lee Canyon, on the other side of Mt. Charleston, is the only ski area in southern Nevada. The best way to reach it in winter is via Lee Canyon Road, SR-156, from U.S. Highway 95. On your way from Las Vegas, don't turn at Kyle Canyon Road, rather, keep going to the next turnoff.

For an off-season look at the ski area as part of your one-day survey, there's a shortcut from Kyle Canyon Road to Lee Canyon. When you come down the mountain from the Mt. Charleston Resort past the ranger station, look for the turnoff to SR-158. From there, it's just six miles to a junction with 156, Lee Canyon Road.

Ski season usually begins after Thanksgiving, but may start earlier or later, depending upon the first snowfall. In summer you can take a ride in one of the chairlifts for sweeping views of the valley and canyons.

In winter this is a playground for Las Vegas snow-birds. The **Lee Canyon Ski Area** has plenty of room for downhill and cross-country skiers and provides free transporation from the city. Some Las Vegans who don't ski at all like to go there just to sit in the sunshine and watch the skiers from the deck of the lodge. Ski slopes and runs are graded for beginners, intermediates, and experts. There's snow-making equipment to help nature, if necessary, and bright lights for night skiing. Snow-boarders are welcome on a special slope, where they won't collide with downhill racers on skis.

Las Vegan Kate Butler says she and her family have been skiing at Lee Canyon for twenty-five years: "No matter how often I visit the ski area," she wrote in *Nevada* magazine, "there always seems to be something new and different—skiers in wild outfits, Las Vegas show people lounging on the deck. . . . Once I chanced upon Siegfried and Roy coaxing two baby tigers onto the chairlift."

If you're heading for the slopes, call ahead for information about conditions; it's a twenty-four-hour number:

Road and snow conditions: (702) 593-9500

For a current ski report: (702) 658-1927

More questions about Lee Canyon? (702) 872-5462

To reach the Lee Canyon Guard Station:
(702) 872-5453

Equipment Rental

Visitors don't have to wrestle their own ski equipment aboard a plane to Las Vegas. Several ski-rental shops in the city will outfit you and your children for a day on the slopes. Some have more than one location and most sell lift tickets too. You'll find them listed in the Yellow Pages. Here are a few suggestions.

McGhies Ski Chalet
4503 West Sahara Avenue
(702) 252-8077
3310 East Flamingo
(702) 433-1120

Nevada Bob's
3131 West Sahara Avenue
(702) 362-9904

Oshman's Sporting Goods
1221 East Sahara Avenue
(702) 732-4173
4300 Meadows Lane
(702) 877-1314

Play It Again Sports
(new and used)
2001 South Rainbow Road
(702) 228-1713
2250 East Tropicana Avenue
(702) 261-9038

Ski Lee Rentals
2395 North Rancho Drive
(702) 646-0008

Chapter 11

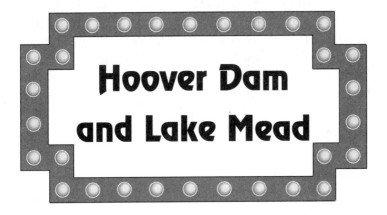

Hoover Dam and Lake Mead

With all the sights and shows and games competing for their attention in Las Vegas, most visitors never see the natural and man-made wonders beyond the city limits. In a recent survey made for the Las Vegas Convention & Visitors Authority, only 29 percent of respondents said they had explored anything outside Las Vegas.

The other 71 percent didn't know what they were missing, but some are gradually finding out. According to the same survey, the number of non-city-bound travelers is up in recent years. Maybe these new adventurers heard intriguing reports from friends who came home with stacks of vacation snapshots: water-skiers skimming across **Lake Mead**, a family group dwarfed by the massive Hoover Dam, a houseboat nestled in a secluded cove at sunset, firelight on faces at a barbecue on the beach, prize photos of bighorn sheep at the edge of a distant cliff.

Among the daring minority who added an outdoor dimension to their Las Vegas vacations, more than half (53 percent) said they had visited **Hoover Dam**, the engineering marvel that first harnessed the capricious power of the Colorado River sixty years ago. Another 28 percent mentioned **Lake Mead**, one of the world's largest artificial lakes, created by Hoover Dam. Statisticians didn't say how many vacationers had visited both, but it's a safe bet that anyone who toured Hoover Dam saw at least part of the lake. Every year some thirteen million tourists visit Hoover Dam. You can follow their example and collect your own vacation memories.

HOOVER DAM

You've seen pictures of this engineering wonder, but somehow photos don't quite prepare you for its *hugeness*. As you glimpse it from the highway for the first time, you suddenly realize that those tiny insects, crawling across the top of a curved wall of concrete, are cars and buses. Drive across it yourself, step out of the car at the Arizona-Nevada border, and look down. You're

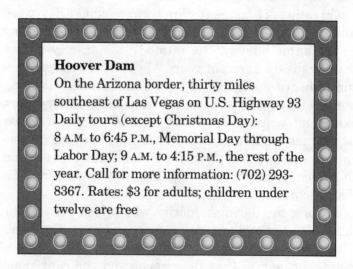

Hoover Dam
On the Arizona border, thirty miles southeast of Las Vegas on U.S. Highway 93
Daily tours (except Christmas Day): 8 A.M. to 6:45 P.M., Memorial Day through Labor Day; 9 A.M. to 4:15 P.M., the rest of the year. Call for more information: (702) 293-8367. Rates: $3 for adults; children under twelve are free

exactly 726.4 feet from the bottom, farther up than you'd be on the roof of a fifty-story skyscraper. Welcome to Hoover Dam, the biggest dam in the world at the time it was constructed, and a model for bigger ones built later in other parts of the world.

You buy tickets for the tour inside the Visitor Center. A rocket-swift elevator takes you down into the cool interior. For the next thirty-five minutes, a guide leads you through tunnels and into cavernous chambers, where towering turbines generate enough electric power to serve three states. In the control room, panels of flashing lights remind you of *Star Trek*.

A concise history of the building of Hoover Dam is part of the guide's commentary. You learn how the dam helped to control the fury of the Colorado River, preventing devastating floods. You find out how it speeded up the development of Las Vegas and southern California by providing cheap electricity. When you hear that the dam contains seven million tons of concrete—enough to pave a two-lane highway from Miami to Los Angeles—the thought is as mind-boggling as all the other statistics: Nine million tons of rock—roughly enough to build the Great Wall of China—had to be excavated to prepare the site. A thousand miles of steel pipe and eighteen million pounds of construction steel—enough for the Empire State Building—are somewhere inside.

At the end of the tour, you'll want to spend a little time wandering around the air-conditioned Visitor Center. In summer the midday temperature outside could be above 100° F, a good reason for starting the day early. Once outside, take a close look at the monumental bronze sculptures at the entrance. Two stylized winged figures sit on thrones of black marble and reach for the sky. When he created the statues in the early 1930s, sculptor Oskar J. W. Hansen said they symbolized the "mental fire, daring, and imagination" of the builders of Hoover Dam.

What's in a Name?

When the dam was being built in the early 1930s, it was called Boulder Dam, authorized by the federal Boulder Canyon Project Act of 1928. Before that, Bureau of Reclamation engineers had spent more than ten years studying possible sites for a dam on the Colorado River and had narrowed their choices down to two: Boulder Canyon and Black Canyon. By the time the act was passed, engineers had selected Black Canyon as the better site, but the earlier name stuck for years.

Herbert Hoover, secretary of commerce under President Calvin Coolidge, was very much involved in the planning of the dam. Long before the Boulder Canyon Project Act was signed, Hoover had worked on complex negotiations among six states and Mexico to secure the Colorado River Compact, the agreement that made possible all later engineering plans for the dam. After Hoover became president in 1928, he continued to support the dam, even though the country was struggling through the Great Depression. So in 1930, Congress acted to name the planned structure Hoover Dam, but the original name was still in common use.

By 1935, when the dam was completed, President Franklin Roosevelt dedicated it as Boulder Dam. Most people called it that until 1947, when President Harry Truman recalled the earlier congressional act and suggested that Hoover's name be restored to the mighty structure. Once again Congress acted, and Boulder Dam became Hoover Dam.

COMMERICAL TOURS

The easiest, most trouble-free way to sample Hoover Dam, Lake Mead, and a few other sights in a limited time is to take a commercial tour, with no worries about maps and timetables. Several companies offer all-day bus tours at reasonable prices. Some combine a bus tour with a cruise on the lake; others throw in a visit to a chocolate factory and a drive past "homes of the stars." One company specializes in river tours, offering adventurous sight-seers a duck's-eye view of Hoover Dam while floating through Black Canyon and down the Colorado River on a raft. Others take you by helicopter or small plane, flying over the dam and Lake Mead and into the Grand Canyon.

Your hotel concierge can recommend packaged excursions, and you'll find a list of tour companies in chapter 15 of this book. Most tour companies advertise in *What's On in Las Vegas* and *Showbiz Weekly,* those free magazines you find in your hotel rooms. Some ads include discount coupons. For quick reference, here are a few possibilities.

Garth Tours takes you to Hoover Dam and includes a Lake Mead cruise on the *Desert Princess* paddle-wheel steamer. Recent price has been $31.90, but call for current ticket information and schedules: (702) 382-2010 or (800) 647-1414.

Gray Line Tours of Southern Nevada lists a similar combination tour, including the lake cruise and a buffet lunch, at $31.60 per person. (At certain times you may receive discount coupons offering this same tour at $49 for two adults.) Gray Line also does a less expensive "Express" tour, twice a day, with two hours at the dam. For reservations and current information, call (702) 384-1234.

Guaranteed Tours offers a six-hour tour to Hoover Dam with a look at stars' homes, a visit to Boulder City, lunch at the Gold Strike Inn, and a stop the Ethel M Chocolate Factory in Henderson—all for $22.95 per person. Confirm this at (702) 369-1000 or (800) 777-6555.

Key Tours advertises a "Hoover Dam Plus" excursion, with stops in Henderson and Boulder City, for $28. Check it out: (702) 362-9355.

Wild West Tour Company joins the others with combination Hoover Dam/Lake Mead cruise packages. Their twenty-four-hour reservation number is (702) 731-2425.

Adventure Airlines adds a flight over Red Rock Canyon to its air-ground-water tour of Hoover Dam, Boulder City, and Lake Mead, which includes a cruise on the *Desert Princess*. Call for schedules and prices: (702) 736-7511.

Lake Mead Air specializes in scenic flights to the Grand Canyon, taking off from Boulder City for a close look at Hoover Dam and the entire length of Lake Mead. Latest price quoted was $89 per person with a minimum of two fares, plus a National Park fee. Call for update: (702) 293-1848.

Scenic Airlines caters to international visitors with multilingual narration and patch cords for video cameras. Price has been $79 for a seventy-five-minute flight over Hoover Dam and Lake Mead. Overnight trips to the Grand Canyon or three-day expeditions to Monument Valley, Utah, are considerably more—up to $429 per person. Check by phone: (702) 739-1900.

Sierra Nevada Airways also offers multilingual all-day tours to the Grand Canyon, flying over Hoover Dam and Lake Mead and then landing in Arizona for a three-hour bus tour through Grand Canyon National Park and a buffet lunch. All this for $125, until prices change.

A quicker flight for visitors in a hurry—two and a half hours from your hotel and back—covers the same aerial view without landing, for $75. Call for reservations: (702) 736-6767.

Sundance Helicopters suggests a champagne picnic inside the Grand Canyon River Gorge after a scenic flight from Las Vegas: $295. They'll give you a custom-tailored itinerary, for a price. Call (702) 736-0606.

Black Canyon Raft Tours will take you down the Colorado River on a big inflated raft, from the base of Hoover Dam to Willow Beach, a four-hour expedition with a picnic lunch along the way. You'll learn about the rocks, wildlife, and history of the place and may even see a few bighorn sheep. Expect to get a bit wet, but the water is relatively calm, no white-water rapids. The cost is $65.95 for those who drive directly to 1297 Boulder Highway, Boulder City; add $5 if you want to be picked up at and returned to your hotel. Call (702) 293-3776.

Lake Mead Cruises

Cruises to Hoover Dam are much tamer (and less expensive) aboard the *Desert Princess,* an air-conditioned, three-story Mississippi paddle wheeler. A year-round family favorite is the daily 9 A.M. breakfast-buffet cruise: $21 for adults and $10 for children. Later morning and afternoon sight-seeing cruises cost $14.50 for adults and $6 for children. No buffet, but the snack bar is always open. There's also an evening dinner/dance cruise, not recommended for young children, and the price is $43 for all ages. These prices apply only if you book your own cruise. Several bus and air tours, listed above, include *Desert Princess* cruises as part of their packages.

For reservations or more information, call (702) 293-6180. If you make your own arrangements, you'll board the *Desert Princess* at the Lake Mead Resort Marina, 322 Lake Shore Road, Boulder City. The Marina telephone number is (702) 293-3484.

Traveling on your own, there's more than one way to reach Lake Mead and Hoover Dam from Las Vegas, depending on your starting point. For most visitors lodged in hotels on or near the Strip, the most popular route is the most direct, taking in the dam, the lake, Boulder City, and Henderson in an easily manageable daytrip.

To make the most of your day, especially during the summer, set out in the cool hours of early morning and allow about forty-five minutes for driving to the dam. (Add an hour or more if you stop in Boulder City on the way.) From the Strip, turn east at any major cross street between Tropicana and Sahara Avenues. When you reach the Boulder Highway (U.S. 93 & 95), turn right and head southeast toward Boulder City. On the way, you'll pass through Henderson, a Las Vegas suburb, where the family can enjoy several free tours and receive free samples of marshmallows, chocolates, and cranberry drinks. (Don't stop now. If you save these places for an afternoon visit on your return trip, you'll appreciate the air-conditioning.)

Right now, if you're heading for Hoover Dam, the first stop on this expedition will be Boulder City . . . unless you'd rather beat the heat and go directly to the dam for an 8 A.M. tour and a brief look at the lake. You could be back in Boulder City in time for lunch.

BOULDER CITY—A MODEL TOWN

You may still hear old-timers call it "Boulder Dam," especially in Boulder City. The town and the dam grew up together, but the town came first. Before any construction could begin on the dam, the Bureau of Reclamation had to figure out a way to bring in more than five thousand workers and all the materials necessary for building the massive structure. Somehow these workers and their families had to be fed and housed near the site. Black Canyon was a genuine wilderness: no houses, no residents, no food or water or electricity—except in Las Vegas, the small railroad town almost forty miles away.

The electric power essential for construction was a lot more power than Las Vegas had ever seen. Poles and wire had to be installed along a two-hundred-mile path to bring electricity from the nearest big power plant in San Bernardino, California. And a town for the workers had to be built from the ground up.

The whole story is told vividly in a movie shown regularly at the town museum. It's worth a visit, even if it delays your arrival at the dam. The movie and other exhibits will help you understand the engineering phenomenon you're about to visit, or appreciate what you've already seen.

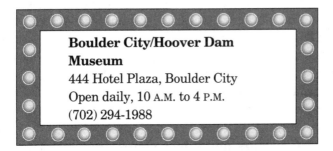

> **Boulder City/Hoover Dam Museum**
> 444 Hotel Plaza, Boulder City
> Open daily, 10 A.M. to 4 P.M.
> (702) 294-1988

Massive pieces of machinery, old photos, historical documents, and all sorts of artifacts from the dam's construction years are preserved in this museum. You'll see earlier photos taken in 1905 and 1906 during a devastating two-year flood, when the untamed Colorado River poured over hundreds of square miles, destroying farms and homes. It was this destruction, and the previous cycle of flood and drought, that led the Bureau of Reclamation to begin studies to harness the awesome power of the river, leading to the construction of Hoover Dam.

Other exhibits trace the history of Boulder City itself, carefully planned as an orderly, secure model town, where everything was owned and operated by the federal government. Strict ordinances prohibiting alcohol and gambling seemed oppressive to some single workers who lived in regimented dormitories. On weekends, after days of backbreaking labor in the blazing heat of Black Canyon, these men often escaped to Las Vegas, where gambling was legal and small nightclubs promised a little gaiety. Even if they emptied their pockets at the tables, they seemed willing to keep coming back to the bright lights of Fremont Street.

As Las Vegas residents watched the dam's progress, they also watched their city grow . . . along with its reputation as a wide-open, Wild West town. Boulder City remained quiet and orderly. After the dam was completed and workers moved away, Boulder City became a tourist attraction, a gateway to the dam, and a service center for vacationers bound for Lake Mead Recreation Area. It was still owned and run by the U.S. Bureau of Reclamation as late as 1960. Since then it has become an independent municipality with its own city charter; a city where residents own their homes and small businesses. Bars and liquor stores are legal now, but gambling is still forbidden. You won't find any casinos in Boulder City.

Across the street from the museum, you'll see the sedate old Boulder Hotel, now refurbished but seeming unchanged for more than half a century. To see more of the town and learn more about its history, pick up some brochures and maps.

Boulder City Chamber of Commerce
1497 Nevada Highway, Boulder City
(702) 293-2034

Here's your best source of local information. Ask about the **Historic District walking tour**. You'll receive a handy map of Boulder City with concise details about numbered places of interest. If you're there in April, you'll hear about the annual **Spring Craft Show**. In October, **Art in the Park** draws crowds to outdoor exhibits. In summer, ask if the bighorn sheep still spend late afternoons in the city park. If the summer is especially hot, the grass dries up in the rocky hills where the sheep live, and they can't find much to eat. Consequently, they may try to escape the heat of the day by napping in caves or any shady spot they can find. Then, in late afternoon, they often come down from the hills to graze in the green park.

If the bighorn sheep are your main reason for coming to Boulder City, you'll want to change your timetable. Late afternoon is the only time you're likely to see them. You might schedule a stop on your return trip from Hoover Dam . . . or a separate visit on another afternoon. Then you'd have time to browse in the shops on Arizona Street and the Nevada Highway. Downtown streets are lined with gift shops, galleries, and boutiques filled with Indian and Mexican crafts and works by local artists. One gallery has expanded to become a mini-museum with a special focus.

Bruno's Indian and Turquoise Museum
1306 Nevada Highway, Boulder City
(702) 293-4865

You'll find authentic Indian lore among paintings, jewelry, and souvenirs at this trading post and art gallery. Paiute artists are there to demonstrate their skill, showing you how they polish turquoise and shape silver into jewelry. In the museum section, two movies and a series of exhibits show how the Ancient Ones lived in the Southwest and how modern Paiutes still preserve their heritage in dance and jewelry making.

If you're on your way to Hoover Dam, you're almost there. If you're heading back to Las Vegas, maybe you and the kids are ready for a refreshing stop in Henderson.

HENDERSON—TOWN OF FREE TOURS AND SWEET SAMPLES

This is an industrial suburb. Factories and warehouses don't look especially inviting from the highway, but side streets lead to tree-shaded neighborhoods of small houses. Several manufacturing and processing plants in Henderson offer hospitality to school groups and any other visitors interested in seeing how their products are made.

Ethel M Chocolate Factory
#2 Cactus Garden Drive, Henderson
Open daily, 8:30 A.M. to 7 P.M. (closed Thanksgiving and Christmas)
Admission is free; for more information call
(702) 458-8864

Chocolate-lovers can watch through big picture windows as white-coated workers, surrounded by polished steel vats and machines, create rich goodies such as truffles, nut clusters, and chocolate-covered mints—and there are free samples in the tasting room. These top-drawer candies are named for Ethel Mars, wife of the tycoon who launched Milky Way, Mars Bars, and M&Ms. Tour buses stop here all day long. Passengers head for the spotless rest rooms, take the tour, nibble chocolates, buy gifts, and wander through the two-acre cactus garden to examine labeled desert plants.

Kidd's Marshmallow Factory
8203 Gibson Road, Henderson
Open daily, 9:30 A.M. to 4:30 P.M.
Admission is free; for more information
call (702) 564-5400

Not just the usual white confections, but marshmallows in unexpected colors and shapes are made here. Pink and orange marshmallows, bigs ones and little ones, and marshmallows with the face of Mickey Mouse are shipped all over the world. See how it's done, from start to finish, in a self-guided tour. Then accept a free bag of marshmallows from Kidd's. The Kidd name, by the way, belongs to the family who owns the factory . . . and they do have six kids.

Cranberry World West
5975 American Pacific Boulevard, Henderson
Open daily, 9 A.M. to 5 P.M.
(702) 566-7160

The newest and biggest of the Henderson show-and-tell displays opened late in 1994 at the $50 million Ocean Spray cranberry processing plant. Instead of taking you into the plant, Ocean Spray has built a separate Visitor Center with a hundred-seat theater, a demonstration kitchen, audiovisuals, and interactive displays to show the cranberry's journey from marshy eastern bogs to finished bottles and jars of cranberry drinks, cranberry mustard, and cranberry jelly. Entertainment includes the dancing "Cran-Cran Girl."

Henderson is less than fifteen miles from the Strip—so close you can get there in a few minutes. Any one of these factory tours can be a spur-of-the-moment excursion during your Las Vegas vacation. No need to feel that "It's now or never" at the end of a full day of sightseeing. Now that you know where to find them, you can keep them in mind for those late-afternoon, a-few-hours-before-the-dinner-show what-do-we-do-now dilemmas.

In the same town, you'll also find an unusual historical museum with especially stylish and imaginative exhibits.

Clark County Heritage Museum
1830 South Boulder Highway, Henderson
Open daily, 9 A.M. to 4:30 P.M.
(702) 455-7955

For historical background on the Las Vegas area, you can't beat the vivid displays in this museum complex. A "time-line" exhibit in the main museum traces twelve thousand years of Native American cultures, from prehistoric times to the present. Outside, explore some old railcars and learn how railroads changed the face of southern Nevada. Then stroll down "Heritage Street," where four original houses and a print shop have been preserved. Not far away, you walk into a crumbling ghost town in the desert. This history lesson is painless and fun for the kids.

LAKE MEAD AT LEISURE

So far you've seen only a small part of Lake Mead National Recreation Area. The whole park covers 1.5

million acres, a territory twice the size of Rhode Island, administered by the National Park Service under the United Stated Department of the Interior. It has an irregular shape, reaching north to the Virgin Mountains, where the Muddy River meets the Virgin River, and south to the Davis Dam (near Laughlin, Nevada, and Bullhead City, Arizona), where a second lake—long, skinny Lake Mohave—is also part of the Lake Mead National Recreation Area. An eastern arm of the park extends all the way to the Grand Canyon in Arizona.

Your one-day, all-purpose trip to Hoover Dam gave you a superficial look at Lake Mead, but there's much more to see. You want to explore hidden coves by boat, climb the rocks, and hike through desert wilderness and sample the fishing, swimming, and picnic spots described in the brochures. You want to photograph wild burros and wildflowers in another season. If somebody in your family is already asking, "When are we coming back?" you'll need some time to plan ahead for a future Lake Mead vacation. But while you're here, the best source of information for the whole recreation area is very close to Hoover Dam.

Alan Bible Visitor Center
601 Nevada Highway (U.S. Highway 93),
Boulder City. Open daily, 8:30 A.M. to
4:30 P.M. (closed Thanksgiving, Christmas,
and New Year's Day) (702) 293-8906

Browse through exhibits showing how nature created this land and how man has changed it. Learn about desert animals and plant life, then explore the small botanical garden outside. Park rangers will answer your questions and show the kids how to qualify as Junior Rangers. (Children who answer all questions on the quiz will receive official badges through the mail.)

Don't pass up the racks of free maps and brochures describing the recreational possibilities in six developed sites on the lake and in the surrounding wilderness. And for future planning, be sure to pick up a copy of the official Lake Mead color map and brochure produced by the National Park Service. It's packed with concise information, including historical notes, wildlife descriptions, and details about swimming, fishing, hiking, and boating. There's a whole section on safety for swimmers, divers, water-skiers, and boaters.

You'll find other free publications, too. They'll tell you about hiking trails and scenic drives, when and where to look for bighorn sheep, and how to identify (and avoid) scorpions, rattlesnakes, and gila monsters. They'll warn you not to hike in summer heat (June through September are best avoided) and to watch out for flash floods on desert roads. Ask for a copy of the *Desert Lake View* newspaper to find emergency numbers, features for children, and valuable advice.

Admission to the Lake Mead National Recreation Area has been free, so far. Beginning in the summer of 1996, visitors will pay a $5 entrance fee. Plans call for nine information booths at the new park gateway, where visitors will be given maps, water updates, and safety precautions. For current information, before you leave home, call or write to:

Superintendent
Lake Mead National Recreation Area
601 Nevada Highway
Boulder City, NV 89005-2426
(702) 293-8906

Boating Opportunities

All sorts of boats pass each other on Lake Mead, from fishing boats and runabouts to twenty-four-foot patio boats and houseboats accommodating up to twelve people. You can rent a fishing boat for as little as $35 for a half day, $60 a day, or $275 a week. A houseboat would cost you from $650 for three days and two nights in the off-season (September to June) to $1,050 for seven days and six nights in summer. These floating homes have become so popular that you have to arrange way in advance to rent one—reservations should be made at least six months ahead of time.

Two commercial boat-rental companies are authorized concessionaires of the National Park Service. Both operate a string of resorts on Lake Mead and Lake Mohave and both have toll-free numbers to call for information. You can also write for details.

Seven Crown Resorts

P.O. Box 16247
Irvine, CA 92713
(800) 752-9669

Seven Crown will send you brochures describing boat rentals, from the three-passenger *Ski-Doo,* a favorite with water-skiers, to the luxurious *Starship Deluxe* and *Sierra 10,* both equipped with bathtubs and showers, microwave ovens, and two-way radios. Seven Crown operates three resorts at Lake Mead. Each has hotel or motel accommodations as well as a boat marina. Ask for information about all three. If you already know which one you prefer, call or write to:

Lake Mead Resort
322 Lakeshore Road
Boulder City, NV 89005
(702) 293-3484; lodge: (702) 293-2074

Echo Bay Resort
Via Star Route #89010
Overton, NV 89040
(702) 394-4066

Temple Bar Resort
P.O. Box 545
Temple Bar, AZ 86443
(602) 767-3211

Forever Resorts
Box 100, HCR-30
Las Vegas, NV 89124
(800) 255-5561; marina: (702) 565-8958

This company operates a resort on Lake Mohave as well as the six-hundred-slip Callville Bay marina on Lake Mead.

For information about sailboats and other small craft, get in touch with **Lake Mead Boat Rentals** at:

Las Vegas Bay Marina
P.O. Box 91150
Henderson, NV 89009
(702) 565-9111

CHAPTER 12

Valley of Fire State Park

Imagine an outdoor sculpture garden covering fifty thousand acres of desert. Fantastic shapes, like otherworldly animals, arches, and caverns, change color as the sun creates moving shadows among them. Human visitors have given names to these sculptures—Elephant Rock, Seven Sisters, Beehives, Rock of Gibraltar—but the artist is nature.

Seeing the Valley of Fire State Park for the first time, some visitors describe a strange feeling that they've been there before. Maybe they *have* seen it in science fiction movies or in the several *Star Trek* episodes that were filmed in this rocky landscape. Since the 1920s, when early Hollywood moviemaker Hal Roach used the Valley of Fire as background for his silent black-and-white westerns, this desert wilderness has been a favorite movie set, versatile enough to represent prehistoric earth or a distant planet.

Today the Nevada Division of State Parks, charged with protecting the fragile desert environment, regulates such commercial uses but hasn't abolished them. Park Supervisor Gary Rimbey says he receives at least three hundred calls a year from movie and television companies wanting permission to film in the park. About a hundred of these ventures receive permits. Others are refused, for various reasons, but especially if they want to build sets that might disturb wildlife or damage rocks and plants.

Rimbey and his staff are especially careful to protect the ancient petroglyphs, drawings carved into rock surfaces by early native wanderers, centuries before the first Europeans arrived. The Valley of Fire is one of the major southwestern sites where such rock art has been preserved.

One enormous rock covered with petroglyphs has been damaged over the years by modern visitors who scrawled or carved their names among the prehistoric symbols. Now the ancient artwork is protected by a Plexiglas shield, installed by park workers in the mid-1980s to allow people to see the petroglyphs without having access to the rock.

Your own excursion to the Valley of Fire can be an easy daytrip from Las Vegas. If you're really in a hurry, it's possible to get there and back in a morning, allowing an hour for driving each way on the freeway and another hour to see some of the park's highlights from your car, but be prepared to want more time.

A full day will allow you to follow an interesting loop route, including the Lost City Museum in Overton, where remains of an ancient pueblo community have been reconstructed. (Part of the original site is now buried under Lake Mead.) You can explore the Northshore Road above the lake, with stops at some of the beaches and marinas. You'll have more time to enjoy exhibits in the Valley of Fire Visitor Center, as well as time to get out of the car for picture taking and short hikes. If the weather is too hot for a picnic lunch, you can take advantage of an air-conditioned restaurant within a few miles of the wilderness. Then you'll have the rest of the afternoon to explore the recreation area. Maybe you'll plan a future camping trip.

EXCURSION TO THE PAST

Have a good breakfast before you start this expedition. Once you're outside the city on Interstate 15 in the Moapa Valley, restaurants aren't easy to find. And be sure to have an accurate road map. Some maps are a little vague about state roads off the freeway. In summer leave Las Vegas early enough to drive the fifty-five miles to the Valley of Fire Visitor Center by 8:30 or 9 A.M, before the sun gets hot enough to fry your skin. Hiking isn't recommended in summer, when temperatures can reach 110° F.

Heading northeast from the Las Vegas Strip toward Utah, look for the turnoff at State Route 169. There are two of these, both on the right, since 169 makes a loop through the park and returns to I-15. If you miss the first turnoff, you'll pass through part of the four-thousand-acre Moapa Indian Reservation. There's a small convenience store near the road, where you can buy snacks, cold drinks, and bottled water to take along, even if you don't plan to hike.

The earlier turnoff will lead you directly to the west entrance to the park. It's open from sunrise to sunset, and there's a small day-use fee for each vehicle. Here you'll find a billboard map and a list of things to see, but a more complete source of information is about four miles ahead. Keep going for a few minutes and you'll see the Visitor Center just off the road. This is the best place to start your sight-seeing.

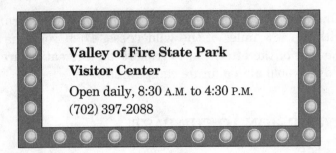

**Valley of Fire State Park
Visitor Center**
Open daily, 8:30 A.M. to 4:30 P.M.
(702) 397-2088

See a film, look at exhibits, browse through bookshelves, and buy a postcard or two. Read about the plants and animals that live among the rocks. Absorb a little history, going back some three hundred million years to a time when the whole region was underwater. Move forward a few million years and imagine a sandy desert with shifting dunes swirled by the wind. As layers of wind-blown sand became solid sandstone, the foundations of the Valley of Fire were laid. Time, sun, water, and chemical action shaped the stone into the marvelous formations you see today. In other parts of the Southwest, the same forces were at work, chiseling the towering cliffs of Red Rock Canyon and Zion National Park in Utah.

Here in the Visitor Center, you'll get a preview of petroglyphs you'll see on some of the rocks outside. You'll learn something about the ancient people who carved these symbols and about later European explorers and pioneers who eventually found their way here. The first rough roads through the Valley of Fire were built in 1914 as part of the Arrowhead Trail between Salt Lake City and Los Angeles. In the early 1930s, the Civilian Conservation Corps built better roads and a few stone shelters. By 1935 the Nevada state legislature established the State Park Commission, and the Valley of Fire became Nevada's first state park.

Before you leave the Visitor Center, take advantage of the drinking fountains and rest rooms while you can, and if you plan to do any hiking, be sure to carry bottled water. Rangers will give you a small brochure full of concise facts about the park, including a few regulations. It's a good idea to read these before you start exploring. The brief list tells you where you can drive, camp, or build cooking fires. Among other requests, you'll be warned: "Please do not remove or disturb any rocks, petrified wood, or other natural objects." And, in case you're traveling with pets, ". . . they must be kept on a leash of not more than six feet in length."

The best part of this brochure is a compact map of the park with places of special interest clearly marked and numbered. Most of these places can be seen from the paved road, or from short stretches of gravel road, without leaving your air-conditioned car. But the best way to *experience* the place is on foot, especially in spring or fall. Even in summer, if you can stand the heat, a few very short walks are possible.

From the parking lot outside the Visitor Center, backtrack to the **Scenic Loop Road**, a two-mile route past some of the park's most photographed formations, including **Arch Rock** and **Piano Rock.** The favorite stop on this loop is **Atlatl Rock**, an art gallery of ancient petroglyphs carved into the dark "desert varnish" coating the rock. Suns, snakes, bighorn sheep, and stick figures of humans are easily recognizable. One figure seems to be using an *atlatl,* a prehistoric spear-launching device used as far back as three thousand years ago.

Some archaeologists believe these petroglyphs may be that old, but others say the drawings are probably later work of the Anasazi, the Ancient Ones, who left the area about A.D. 1150. Still other scientists give credit to all the early visitors who came through the valley and left messages on this ancient bulletin board. Some artists may have been Paiutes, ancestors of modern Native Americans now living in Las Vegas and the Moapa area.

For a closer look at the petroglyphs on Atlatl Rock, you can climb a spindly stairway (sturdier than it looks) and photograph them through the protective Plexiglas. Your own interpretations of the symbols are probably as accurate as anybody's, but one of the drawings looks like a stepladder. Could that explain how prehistoric artists climbed up to leave their marks? From a stable platform at the top of the present stairway, you'll have a sweeping view of the valley. There's a protective rail, but hold on to small children.

Back in the car, complete the scenic loop and turn left at the western end. Head east and look for a campground. From here you have a good view of the **Beehives**, sandstone domes eroded into shape by wind and water. Keep going east and you'll see a sign pointing to **Petrified Logs**. A short interpretive trail leads to a graveyard of logs and stumps washed in from ancient forests some 225 million years ago, now turned to glassy stone. It's worth getting out of the car to follow the trail, even in blistering heat.

Return to the Visitor Center turnoff and follow a paved side road to the **Petroglyph Canyon Trail** leading to **Mouse's Tank**. The well-marked trail is a half-mile round trip, and there's some shade among the rocks. If you plan to do just one hike in the Valley of Fire, this may be your best bet. You'll see more rock drawings, carefully preserved and just out of reach. At Mouse's Tank, you'll find a marker telling the story of an outlaw Indian called Mouse, who made this canyon his hideout from the police in the 1890s. Rainwater collected in "Mouse's Tank," a natural basin of rock, may have helped him survive.

Keep driving up the same road and you'll come to **Rainbow Vista**, named for the many-colored sandstone hills spread out in the distance. You'll be glad you loaded the camera with color film. The pavement ends here, but a gravel road leads off to the right toward the bright red sandstone of **Fire Canyon** and a weathered sculpture called **Silica Dome**, another prize view for photographers. A three-mile round-trip walk from Rainbow Vista gets you there and back (but not when the thermometer reads 120° F).

Another view from Rainbow Vista is the **White Domes Area**, a place to watch for shadows and changing colors in the sandstone hills. When you put away your camera, you may be tempted to walk toward the domes for a closer look, but it's farther away than it looks—a vigorous seven-mile hike for a spring or autumn visit, not a casual stroll in summer. Certainly not for small children.

Park rangers warn you to carry plenty of water and report to the Visitor Center before going out on foot in this area. Three hours in the sun could be dangerous on a hot day. By car, you can still bump along the gravel road to see exotic plants and colored sandstone in the White Domes Area.

Drive back past the Visitor Center and turn left on State Route 169, the main road through the park. On your right, you'll see the **Seven Sisters**, towering red pillars of rock casting shadows on picnic tables. On the other side of the road, a little farther on, look for **The Cabins**, a row of stone shelters built by the Civilian Conservation Corps in the early 1930s. Now they are part of another picnic area.

Just before leaving the park, you'll recognize the much photographed **Elephant Rock**, that fiery red animal shape that decorates book jackets and illustrates articles about the Valley of Fire. If the kids want a closer look, stop the car and bring out the camera to record one more vacation memory.

So far, unless you stopped often for hiking, you've spent less than two hours in the Valley of Fire, seeing much of it from the car. Families who love the outdoors may be talking about a future visit when the season is right for camping and hiking. No overnight backpacking is allowed in the park, but two campgrounds are equipped with restrooms, water, barbecue grills, and picnic tables. The fifty-one campsites accommodate both tents and motor homes. Experienced Valley of Fire campers say that the best times to see the park are at sunrise and sunset, when shadows are sharp and dramatic.

Rangers will tell you that the best season for hiking is November through March. Spring is the busiest season, and fall is almost as popular. The park has less traffic in summer and winter because of extreme temperatures and flash floods. You can sign up in advance for guided group hikes in the best seasons. When planning a trip to Valley of Fire, write or phone ahead for more information:

Valley of Fire State Park
P.O. Box 515
Overton, NV 89040
(702) 397-2088

or:

Nevada Division of State Parks
Capital Complex or 123 West Nye Lane
Carson City, NV 89710
(702) 687-4370

On your way out, at the **East Entrance Station**, you'll find restrooms and a mounted map to remind you where you are. Where you go next will depend upon whether you turn right or left after leaving the park. This decision may call for a family conference. What time is it? Who's hungry?

What are the possible choices? Turn right and you'll head back to Las Vegas on State Route 167, the scenic **Northshore Road** above Lake Mead. Turn left and you're still on SR-169, bound for **Overton** and the **Lost City Museum**. If you can't make up your mind, follow the signs to Overton Beach on the lakeshore. You'll find a ranger station at the marina to provide maps and advice.

Unless everybody is too tired and hungry for more sight-seeing, it's possible to explore in both directions before the day ends. Assuming you started out really early in the morning, reaching the Visitor Center at 8:30 or 9, and if you spent no more than two hours exploring the Valley of Fire, there's still time for a visit to the Lost City Museum before lunch.

CLUES TO A LOST CULTURE

As you drive the short distance to the Lost City Museum, imagine a time—more than a thousand years ago—when a Pueblo Indian civilization flourished in the Moapa Valley and on the banks of the Muddy River. Centuries before any white man had seen the American continent, before he even knew it existed, pueblo dwellers in this valley were raising maize and cotton, mining salt and turquoise, and trading with neighboring tribes. The **Pueblo Grande de Nevada** was a sophisticated society based on agriculture, developed over the centuries from a culture of wanderering hunters and gatherers.

The road takes you beyond the northern tip of Lake Mead, along the edge of the recreation area, toward farmland in the Muddy River valley. Just before you reach Overton, you'll find a museum where a rare treasury of human history is preserved.

The Lost City Museum
721 South Moapa Valley Boulevard
Overton, NV 89040
Open daily, 8:30 A.M. to 4:30 P.M.
(702) 397-2193

At one time, around A.D. 800, dozens of pueblo villages filled the V-shaped valley where the Muddy and Virgin Rivers converge. The village that stood near this museum site wasn't entirely "lost," but part of it was drowned by Lake Mead in 1935, when Hoover Dam created the lake. As early as 1867, an article in the *New York Tribune* reported a research expedition's discovery of the "ruins of an ancient city" in Nevada. Investigators began to call it the Lost City. Surrounded by desert, the ruins were in a fertile valley where Mormon farmers from Utah were beginning to settle. Long before that, the explorer Jedediah Smith had mentioned these ruins in reports of his travels during the 1820s.

Archaeologists were interested, but nobody attempted a full-scale scientific dig until 1924, when Governor James Scrugham of Nevada organized a research team. Once they started digging, scientists uncovered baskets, pottery, ancient weapons, animal bones, bits of blankets—all sorts of clues to the everyday lives of an ancient people. Most exciting of all were the buildings—

pueblos—prehistoric condominiums that may have housed as many twenty families.

After ten years of careful, systematic excavation, archaeologists felt they had just begun their research. By 1934 they were feeling a little nervous about the construction of Hoover Dam. The new lake would almost certainly submerge at least part of their excavation site. At that point, the Franklin D. Roosevelt administration stepped in, and the Civilian Conservation Corps built a museum in Overton to house the precious collection of Indian artifacts.

Today you'll find the story of an ancient culture vividly presented inside and outside the museum building. On the grounds, several pueblo houses have been reconstructed on original foundations. A small garden displays mesquite, squash, screwbean, and other plants these pueblo dwellers might have gathered or grown.

In front of the museum building, a primitive pit house has been dug to show how nomadic people protected themselves from the intense desert heat, long before the pueblo builders arrived. Archaeologists believe such underground shelters were common in the Valley of Fire area sometime between 300 B.C. and A.D. 700. Here at the Lost City Museum, you can climb down a crude ladder into the pit and imagine what home was like for a prehistoric nomad returning from the hunt with meat for dinner: a rabbit, bird, lizard, or bighorn sheep.

Displays inside the museum trace at least ten thousand years of Nevada history. You'll see tightly woven baskets, clay pottery, and arrowheads made a thousand years ago or more. You'll learn about the Anasazi people, who came to the valley around A.D. 500 and left abruptly 650 years later. Nobody knows why they left so suddenly, but archaeologists speculate that drought, floods, or a disease epidemic may have driven them out of their prosperous farming community. The Paiutes, who came here around A.D. 1000, survived whatever disaster it was that drove the Anasazi away. Modern descendants of these early Paiutes still live in the Moapa Valley.

A fascinating series of photographs in the museum shows the excavation of the Lost City site in 1924. That site is now underwater, along with several more modern small towns flooded in 1935 by the new Lake Mead. Another display interprets some of the petroglyphs found in the Valley of Fire. More petroglyphs are preserved outside.

More-recent excavations in the Moapa Valley are constantly in progress. Some begin almost accidentally when someone digs a foundation for a new house and turns up reminders of past residents. As recently as 1975, an ancient village was uncovered by utility workers digging for a new pipeline. Museum curators will tell you that there are more ruins still buried for miles along the valley. Archaeologists of the future—maybe someone in your family—will discover new details about early inhabitants of the Lost City and their neighbors.

THE HAUNTED LAKE

Some of the ghostliest ghost towns in Nevada are underwater, just a few miles from Overton. Others are still dry but deserted. Small communities, such as St. Thomas and Junction City, were evacuated and then simply disappeared when the Hoover Dam plugged the Colorado River and created Lake Mead. You won't find these names on your current road map, but old-timers in Overton can tell you where they were.

Kaolin, just three miles southeast of Overton, started later than the other two towns. Its history was short, but it survived until just before Hoover Dam was completed. First settled in 1910 by Armenian farmers, Kaolin was named for the chalky mineral being mined in the neighborhood. By 1914 the town had a post office, and by 1930 there were a hundred residents. Four years later, afraid their farms were about to be flooded by Lake Mead, farmers moved out. Some settled in Overton. As it turned out, Kaolin wasn't submerged by the lake, but the town was dead nevertheless.

St. Thomas, about six miles farther south, had prospered off and on since 1864, when Mormon colonists first came over from Utah to plant crops. Seventy years later, the town was evacuated, farms were flooded by Lake Mead, and St. Thomas was no more . . . except sometimes. In very dry seasons, when the water is low, boaters on the lake near Overton Beach see mud-covered stairways and foundations of houses long gone. Gradually, part of the town emerges from the depths. When the rains come, St. Thomas disappears once more. Divers occasionally explore the underwater town-site, stirring up the ghosts.

Junction City died long before it was flooded, but the ruins still exist at the bottom of the lake, near the south end of the Overton arm. Mormon farmers first settled Junction City in 1869, but they left when confronted by Indians protesting, sometimes violently, the invasion of land they had occupied for centuries. White travelers returned to the place a few years later, when Nevada gold seekers, bound for Arizona mines, came there to cross the Colorado River on Daniel Bonelli's ferryboat.

The enterprising Bonelli found the ferry business so profitable that he built an inn, established a farm, and employed local Indians to help him run his businesses. The settlement grew and was renamed **Rioville** when a post office opened in 1881. Over the next twenty-five years, Bonelli kept the place going, even after new railroads diverted traffic from his ferry and the boat was destroyed. After Bonelli died in 1904, Rioville survived another two years before the post office closed. It was already a ghost town before its underwater burial. You can't see it, but you know it's there.

History buffs will find several books about Nevada ghost towns in libraries and bookstores. Almost all of them mention Stanley Paher's *Nevada Ghost Towns and Mining Camps* as their basic source. Illustrated with old photographs from several western archives, Paher's 1970 guidebook is still the most complete reference on these extinct communities. His more recent supplementary atlases, published in paperback, help ghost town explorers find their way around. Another favorite reference, compact enough to carry in your pocket, is the *Ghost Towns and Historic Sites* map, published by *Nevada* magazine.

RETURN TRIP ON THE NORTHSHORE ROAD

After a strenuous morning of sight-seeing in the Valley of Fire and the Lost City Museum, you'll be more than ready for lunch. Some travelers stop in Overton to eat or buy picnic supplies. Whether you're counting on an outdoor picnic or a full meal in an air-conditioned restaurant, you can find both on your way back to Las Vegas along the Northshore Road.

About twelve miles south of Overton you'll see **Blue Point Spring**, the first of two picnic spots with tables.

A little farther along, you'll come to **Rogers Spring**, a popular oasis with a short scenic trail leading up to a gorgeous view. Be sure to bring your own drinking water if you picnic at either of these places. The warm springs look pretty, but don't drink the water.

Air-conditioned comfort is not far away. A few miles south of Rogers Spring, turn off the road toward **Echo Bay**. The **Tail o' the Whale** restaurant at Seven Crown's Echo Bay Resort will serve you a sturdy or light lunch with a view of Lake Mead. Afterward you can stroll down to the bustling marina for a look at the houseboats. Impulsive water-skiers might ask about a spur-of-the-moment ski-boat rental. And if you're thinking about a future trip to Lake Mead, now's the time to check out the lakeshore hotel at Echo Bay or look into reserving a houseboat.

By this time, the family may be ready to start back to Las Vegas for a nap or a swim in the hotel pool. It's a sixty-mile drive from Echo Bay, slightly longer than your direct route to the Valley of Fire on Interstate 15. On the Northshore Road, you'll pass more picnic spots, trailheads for hikes, and signs directing you to **Callville Bay**, another big marina. To get a list of Northshore short hikes, write or call:

Lake Mead National Recreation Area
601 Nevada Highway
Boulder City, NV 89005-2426
(702) 293-8906

Stay on SR-167, the Northshore Road, until it joins SR-147. This will take you right back to Las Vegas and the Strip. After a good night's sleep, you'll be ready for another desert adventure.

CHAPTER 13

Laughlin and Lake Mohave

"Thirty years ago," the Laughlin taxi driver tells you, "there were more coyotes than people in this town . . . and it wasn't even a town."

Sounds like a tall Nevada tale, but it's true. Before 1977 Laughlin wasn't on the map. Eleven years earlier, down in the skinny southernmost tip of the state, there was nothing at this spot on the west bank of the Colorado River except a lonely roadside diner, a deserted eight-room motel, and a bait shop.

The diner had opened around 1949 to serve construction crews at work on the Davis Dam, a hundred miles south of Las Vegas. Most of the workers lived across the river in Bullhead City, Arizona, but a construction camp called South Point was set up on the Nevada side. After the dam was completed in 1953, everybody left the camp, and South Point didn't see much traffic except for occasional fishermen or curious travelers venturing off the main roads between Los Angeles and the Grand Canyon.

Today the site of the former diner looks like a short section of the Las Vegas Strip. A string of shiny casinos stretches along the riverbank. Every night the Colorado River becomes a glittering light show of colored reflections as it flows past. And every year, swarms of visitors come to fill more than eight thousand hotel rooms. Bargain prices attract Las Vegas residents as well as out-of-state tourists. Most of the casinos operate free ferryboats to bring daytrippers across from the Arizona side, all day and all night.

All this prosperity grew out of Don Laughlin's optimistic imagination. He was thirty-three when he came to South Point and bought the derelict diner along with six acres of land. With a Nevada gaming license and some money he had made in Las Vegas, Laughlin planned to build a modest casino on the property. Because casinos were illegal in Arizona, he thought his place might attract gamblers from Bullhead City, just across the river. By 1966 Laughlin's brand-new Riverside Casino was open, and customers were lining up in a parking lot on the Arizona side, waiting for the free ferry service.

It was a small, informal operation at first. Californians came in from nearby Needles, then others turned up from more distant cities like Barstow and San Bernardino. Across the river in Arizona, Bullhead City was growing fast, and Don Laughlin's Riverside Casino became a sort of unofficial out-of-state suburb. More Arizonans poured in from as far away as Kingman and Flagstaff. The Riverside expanded, and Laughlin's success attracted other entrepreneurs who built their own casinos along the riverbank.

LAUGHLIN—NEW TOWN ON THE MAP

The place had no official name until 1977, when the post office put up a sign for Laughlin, Nevada. By that time, the Riverside had 100 rooms. Seven years later, it had 350 rooms and competition from a half-dozen other casinos. The name of Laughlin began to turn up on national TV weather reports as "the hottest spot in the nation" with summer temperatures constantly above 110° F.

It may have seemed an unlikely location for a cluster of successful resorts—even more unlikely for a real town—but today behind Casino Drive there are houses, condominiums, shopping centers, a medical center, a school, and a library. The resident population has exceeded three thousand and is still growing. There's even a Seniors Association for retired people who have moved here from colder climates.

Your plans for a family vacation in Las Vegas may not extend this far south, but you'll be offered plenty of opportunities to see Laughlin. It's a bright, sunny town with lots of things for families to do. Several tour companies distribute brochures, describing daily bus trips from Las Vegas to the southern city. You'll find some of these leaflets at the concierge desk of your hotel, and others will be handed to you on the street.

Some advertised prices seem too good to be true. "Laughlin Getaway, $5 per person," says one magazine ad, promising round-trip transportation (two hours each way) and six hours of fun in "the newest hot spot in Nevada." The tour includes complimentary lunch and a "fun book" full of discount coupons. Another company recently advertised a two-for-one special fare, $5 per couple, for a similar ten-hour tour with freebies. For a while, one Las Vegas tour operator offered a "free Laughlin fun bus."

It doesn't take long to figure out why the prices are so low. Notice which casinos offer the free lunches and coupons and you'll have a clue. Your casino host is hoping you'll leave some of your money behind at the gaming tables or slots. Children aren't allowed in gambling areas, of course, but most casinos provide other attractions, and there's plenty to do in and around Laughlin.

Ferryboat rides are fun. There are sandy beaches, train rides, and narrated sight-seeing tours aboard air-conditioned riverboats. When the temperature drops below sizzling, you can hike in **Grapevine Canyon** and look for petroglyphs. On the Arizona side, there's a pleasant park and museum. An entertaining ghost town south of Bullhead City has been revived as a tourist attraction, where wild burros still wander through the streets. Davis Dam offers public tours. Lake Mohave, at the southern end of the Lake Mead National Recreation Area, provides a long list of water sports.

BARGAIN TOURS FROM LAS VEGAS TO LAUGHLIN

If you have time for a daytrip to Laughlin, you can't beat the prices of tours offered by the following companies.

Gray Line Tours of Southern Nevada recently listed two daily tours to Laughlin at $7.95 per person, including lunch. They'll pick you up at your Las Vegas hotel at 8 A.M. and bring you back about 4:30 P.M. Or you can leave at noon and return around 8:30 P.M. On the way, the bus passes through Searchlight, an old mining town where gold was discovered in 1897. Once you're in

Laughlin, the tour operator promises plenty of free time to explore and browse on your own. A Gray Line leaflet assures you that "it is not a gambling junket, and there are no time requirements at any of the resorts you may visit." For reservations and current information call (702) 384-1234.

Garth Tours takes you to Laughlin along a similar route for $8, with free lunch and time to find your own entertainment. On a longer tour in the same direction and for a higher price, this company will take you to Laughlin, Lake Havasu, and London Bridge. (It really is the old London Bridge, transported from the Thames to the Arizona desert.) Call for current ticket information and schedules: (702) 382-2010 or (800) 647-1414.

Ray and Ross Transport buses join the daily parade between Las Vegas and Laughlin. The $8 price tag for their tour includes lunch, making it a popular choice. For times and itineraries call (702) 646-4661.

Several other companies advertise $5 tours to Laughlin, with free lunch and coupon books. Among these are:

Guaranteed Tours (702) 369-1000
Key Tours (702) 362-9355
Sightseeing Specialists (702) 383-4010

Special tours of back roads and ghost towns can be arranged for smaller groups through **Old West Territory Tours**, operating out of Oatman, Arizona. They'll pick you up at your Las Vegas hotel in an eight-passenger 4 × 4 or a stretch safari suburban van with room for fourteen passengers. Schedules, itineraries, and prices vary, but the usual backroad tour to Laughlin and Oatman costs around $69.

Oatman, once a prosperous gold-mining center, is a resurrected ghost town, twenty-three miles southeast of Bullhead City, where wild burros mingle with tourists,

and weekend gunfights are staged as Wild West entertainment. History and souvenir shops are plentiful.
Phone for information or reservations: (702) 454-5555 or
(702) 371-2011. The Arizona number is (602) 768-7787.

If your kids would like to see the Colorado River
city with other children in the six-to-sixteen age group,
away from parents, call **Kidz Adventure Tours** in
Henderson. Trained chaperones, licensed by the Public
Service Commission, take groups of young travelers on
all-day excursions to Laughlin with a flexible itinerary of
things to see and do. The $110 price tag includes every-
thing—meals, boat tickets, admissions to museums, souvenir T-shirts, and beepers for keeping track of parents.
Call (702) 564-6631.

GETTING TO LAUGHLIN
WITHOUT A GUIDE

You don't have to take a package tour to get to Laughlin
by bus. **Greyhound Bus Lines** and **K-T Services**
operate daily buses to Laughlin and Bullhead City from
the downtown Las Vegas terminal at Main Street and
Carson Avenue. For current fares and schedules, call
Greyhound's twenty-four-hour number: (800) 231-2222.
For K-T information, call (702) 644-2233.

Families who'd rather plan their own schedules and
itineraries can make the two-hour drive any time they
like, but the American Automobile Association advises
caution, especially in summer. A full page of "Desert
Driving Hints" is included in a special guidebook, *Las
Vegas and Laughlin, Nevada,* published by the Automobile Club of Southern California (pages 218–219).

Hints include specific reminders to carry at least five
gallons of clean water and to fill up with gasoline when-
ever you see a service station (you won't see many).

They'll warn you to check your car's engine, cooling system, and tires before you start out, and they'll tell you what to do if the car becomes disabled in the desert. Even if you already have the current *AAA California/ Nevada Tour Book,* ask for this smaller Las Vegas guide too. It's full of useful tips and details.

If you're driving to Laughlin from Las Vegas, just follow U.S. 95/93 (Boulder Highway) to Boulder City, then head south on 95 toward Needles, California. It's all desert until you reach **Searchlight**, about fifty-five miles south of the city, at the junction with Nevada State Route 164. A brief stop in Searchlight will give you a chance to absorb a little history.

Once upon a time, Searchlight was the biggest town in southern Nevada. At a time when Las Vegas had fewer than twenty-five hundred residents, Searchlight had twice as many, a population of five thousand. Gold, discovered here in 1897, had brought prospectors, investors, and prosperity. Ten years after the first gold strike, the town had forty-four active mines, a short narrow-gauge railway moving ore to the mills, and a business street with thirteen saloons. Local news was reported by two weekly newspapers—the *Bulletin* and the *News*.

This prosperity didn't last. After 1907 the gold began to play out, and Searchlight gradually became a living ghost town. A few people still live here, but ghosts of the past outnumber them, even among modern buildings. You'll find traces of the boom years in the abandoned mines and the skeletons of old miners' shacks scattered around the hills. Searchlight still has a few services for travelers on U.S. 95.

If you turn east at Searchlight on Nevada State Route 164, you'll reach **Cottonwood Cove** on Lake Mohave.

(We'll explore the lake later in this chapter.) For now, keep going south on U.S. 95 and you're on your way to Laughlin. When you reach State Highway 163, turn east toward Laughlin, Bullhead City, Davis Dam, and the southern tip of Lake Mohave. Before you reach the dam, turn right at Laughlin Civic Drive.

See Laughlin and Keep Cool

When you see the **Riverside Resort**, straight ahead, you've found Casino Drive. The **Visitor's Bureau** is to the left, the **Chamber of Commerce** to the right. Drive along the Laughlin "Strip" and you'll pass a string of big resorts, lined up for about three miles between the **Flamingo Hilton** and **Harrah's Laughlin**. In between you'll notice the **Regency**, **Edgewater**, and **Colorado Belle**, the one that looks like a huge, illuminated riverboat. **Ramada Express** is across the street, and the **Golden Nugget** dominates the shore between the **Pioneer** and **Gold River**.

The best way to see the area's highlights in a short time is to take a narrated cruise on an air-conditioned riverboat. Several companies offer frequent one-hour tours priced at around $10 for adults, $6 for children.

Laughlin River Tours, Inc., operates two Mark Twain–style side-wheelers with air-conditioned lower decks and open-air upper decks. Each boat carries 150 passengers and has a snack bar and beverage service. The *Fiesta Queen* departs from Harrah's boat dock six times a day, beginning at 11:30 A.M., with the last cruise at 6:30 P.M. The *Little Belle* leaves from the Edgewater boat dock on about the same schedule as the *Fiesta Queen*, another six cruises daily. Each riverboat follows a leisurely course up and down the river between Laughlin and Bullhead City. Ticket booths are at the boat docks. For more information about Laughlin River Tours, call (702) 298-1047. The direct line to the Edgewater boat dock is (702) 298-2453, extension 3877.

USS *Riverside*—a cruiser-yacht designed to pass safely under the Laughlin–Bullhead City bridge—offers a slightly longer tour, an hour and fifteen minutes, which includes a look at Davis Dam. Departing from the Riverside Casino boat dock five times a day, Monday through Friday (six times on Saturday), the cruises begin every two hours, starting at 10:30 A.M. The latest cruise leaves at 6:30 P.M. on weekdays and 8:30 P.M. on Saturdays. The ticket booth is inside the casino on the ground level, near the door to the boat dock. For more details, call (702) 298-2535, extension 5770.

Easy Excursion from Laughlin

Blue River Safaris offers an unusual all-day tour by bus and boat to **London Bridge**. This is too long to include in a one-day excursion from Las Vegas but is easily manageable if you're staying overnight in Laughlin. Daily tours leave the Colorado Belle Casino boat dock at 9:30 A.M. and return about eight hours later. A tour bus takes you to Park Moabi marina on Lake Havasu, Arizona, where you climb aboard a forty-foot jet cruiser for the water trip through Topack Gorge to **Lake Havasu City**. When you see pennants flying from an old stone bridge, you're almost there.

British travelers who remember the old London Bridge at home will assure you that this is the same bridge that spanned the Thames until the 1960s. When this bridge was replaced by a new one in London, the demolished original was bought by an American real-estate developer and shipped, stone by stone, to Arizona.

Now it connects Lake Havasu City with Pittsburg Point, a state recreation park on an island in Lake Havasu. You'll dock on the mainland side of the bridge near a Tudor-style English village with shops and pubs along the water's edge. After two hours for lunch and shopping, you'll head back to Laughlin by bus through **Oatman**, the once-deserted mining town on historic **Route 66**. (This was the road traveled in the 1930s by hundreds of hopeful refugees fleeing drought in the midwestern dust bowl.) Your bus returns to the Colorado Belle dock around 5:30 P.M. The tour price has been $60, including lunch, but you can check the latest rate by calling Blue River Safaris at (702) 298-0910 or (800) 345-8990.

ENTERING BULLHEAD CITY— WHAT TIME IS IT?

When you cross the river to Bullhead City, you may find yourself looking at clocks and wondering if your watch is right. Nevada is on Pacific time; Arizona is an hour later on Mountain time. The difference gets particularly confusing during daylight saving time. Parts of Arizona ignore the change, so clocks in Laughlin agree with those in Bullhead City during DST. Just make sure you know which clock to watch if you have an appointment on one side or the other.

Free ferryboats will take you across the river from any of the casinos to Bullhead City and back, or you can walk across the bridge. If the weather is too hot for much sight-seeing on foot, catch a shuttle bus on Casino Drive and ride across. Taxis are easy to find at the casinos, or you can call one of Laughlin's two cab companies:

Desert Taxi (702) 298-7575

Lucky Taxi (702) 298-2299

Bullhead City has more choices. To summon a taxi for the return trip, call a dispatcher at:

Desert Taxi (602) 763-0365

Lucky Taxi (602) 754-1100 or (602) 763-7200

Checker Cabs (602) 754-4444

Yellow Cabs (602) 754-1111

On the Arizona side, just north of the bridge, the **Colorado River Museum** is worth a visit. The unusual old building was originally a Catholic church, built in 1947 when Davis Dam was being constructed. Inside you'll see geologic maps of the area and historical exhibits, including old photographs, a piano brought around Cape Horn by ship in 1864, and an anchor from one of the steamboats that used to travel up and down the Colorado River. There's also a miniature model of old Fort Mohave as it was in the late 1800s. The museum is open Tuesday through Saturday, 10 A.M. to 3 P.M. The phone number is (602) 754-3399.

North of the museum, **Davis Camp County Park** stretches along the river, spacious enough for camping, fishing, and hiking as well as swimming and rubber-rafting from a sandy beach. A hike into the marshy south section of the park may give you a surprise view of birds you don't expect to see in the desert—pelicans, geese, herons, gulls, and cormorants. If you plan to fish here, you'll need a license. For more information about the park, call (602) 754-4606.

At the north edge of the park you come to the **Davis Dam**, as vital to this region as Hoover Dam is to other parts of the Southwest. Designed to control floods and droughts in the lower Colorado River lands as far south as Mexico, the dam also provides hydroelectric power for industry and homes. You can tour the powerhouse any day between 7:30 A.M. and 3:30 P.M., Arizona time. It's a free self-guided tour through the plant with maps and a brief recorded lecture. The phone number is (602) 754-3628.

Vacationers see Davis Dam as the southern boundary of **Lake Mohave** in the **Lake Mead National Recreation Area** that extends more than a hundred miles to the north. From the top of the dam, you look across the southern end of Lake Mohave toward **Katherine Landing**, where water-skiers and other pleasure boaters keep the marina busy at the **Lake Mohave Resort**. There's a National Park Service ranger station over there and a campground nearby. When you see a couple of houseboats floating into the middle of the narrow lake, you may start thinking about a future visit to Lake Mohave when you can stay longer.

LAKE MOHAVE—NOW OR LATER?

It's smaller than Lake Mead, and the scenery is a little less rugged at the southern end, but Lake Mohave has its share of desert beauty and recreational variety. Sports fishermen love it. They come from all over the world to angle for game fish such as wide-mouth bass and rainbow trout. The U.S. Fish and Wildlife Hatchery at Willow Beach (about fifteen miles south of Hoover Dam) operates a year-round trout-stocking program for Lake Mohave, and the Nevada Fish and Game Department stocks both lakes with catfish, striped bass, perch, and black crappie.

Narrow Lake Mohave, sixty-seven miles long from Hoover Dam to Davis Dam, is only four miles across at its widest point south of **Cottonwood Cove**. It looks more like a river than a lake north of Cottonwood. Some parts of the lake are no wider than the river was before it was dammed, but Lake Mohave offers vacationers the same kind of activities they find at Lake Mead. Houseboaters, campers, and hikers discover quiet coves. Road travelers find comfortable resorts with swimming beaches, boat ramps, and marinas. National Park rangers provide maps and guidance. Nature provides incomparable scenery.

While you're in Laughlin, you're close enough to Katherine Landing to look in at the **Lake Mohave Resort**. It's operated by Seven Crown Resorts, the same company responsible for the Echo Bay Resort on Lake Mead. There's a similar motel and RV park, a nautical restaurant, and a marina full of boats to rent by the hour, day, or week. Houseboaters plan ahead to rent a luxurious *Starship Deluxe* or a smaller *Crownship 6*, with its own generator, air conditioner, and fully equipped kitchen. For future reference, you can pick up a brochure now or write or call later from home:

Seven Crown Resorts
P.O. Box 16247
Irvine, CA 92713
(800) 752-9669

Or directly to:

Lake Mohave Resort
Katherine Landing
Bullhead City, AZ 86430
(602) 754-3245

When you're driving back to Las Vegas, you'll notice an unpaved road leading off to the right, just a few minutes after you turn onto State Route 163 from Laughlin Civic Drive. If you have enough energy and daylight left for more exploring, you can follow this road to **Grapevine Canyon**. In the shadow of Spirit Mountain, a sacred place for early Mohave Indians, you'll find prehistoric rock carvings on the canyon walls. A small cave near the parking area has been excavated by archaeologists who believe the area was used by ancestors of modern Mohaves and Paiutes as early as A.D. 1100. The canyon is a surprising desert oasis with a small spring, lush plants, and marked hiking trails. When you leave Grapevine Canyon, there's no need to backtrack. Continue on through Christmas Tree Pass to U.S. Highway 95, your direct return route to Las Vegas. The canyon is part of Lake Mead National Recreation Area, so you can request more information from:

Superintendent
Lake Mead National Recreation Area
601 Nevada Highway
Boulder City, NV 89005-2426
(702) 293-8906

One more stop on the road back to Las Vegas could be at **Cottonwood Cove**, another favorite home port for fishermen and houseboaters. **Forever Resorts** of Las Vegas operates a marina here with a motel, RV park, and campground. All sorts of powerboats are available for rent by the hour or day. Spacious *Forever 10* houseboats—with five queen-sized beds, bath, kitchen, and television—are rented by the night with a three-night minimum. The motel has a volleyball court and swimming beach.

If you want to see it now, turn right at Searchlight and follow State Route 164 to the Cove. To send for information, call or write:

Forever Resorts
P.O. Box 100, HCR-30
Las Vegas, NV 89124
(800) 255-5561

You can also write directly to:

Cottonwood Cove Marina
Lake Mohave
P.O. Box 1000
Cottonwood Cove, NV 89046

Back in Las Vegas, you'll be ready to rest. Meanwhile, there are a few practical things to think about before leaving home.

3

Practical Matters

CHAPTER 14

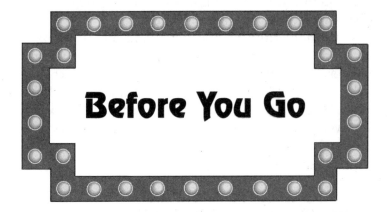

Before You Go

A spur-of-the-moment vacation can be fun, but a little advance planning saves a lot of time and money, especially when Las Vegas is your destination—and especially when you're traveling with kids. More than 25 million people visit Las Vegas every year. The Las Vegas Convention & Visitors Authority reported 28.2 million in 1994 with 31 million expected in 1995. At least 2 million of these visitors are children. If you and your family plan to join the crowd, you'll enjoy it more if you do some homework first.

A few more statistics: At least sixty-one different air carriers bring vacationers into Las Vegas on direct flights from cities in the United States. International charter flights arrive weekly from Germany and, more often, from Mexico and Canada. A nonstop charter service from Manchester, England, began in 1995. On an average day, some 851 flights arrive at McCarran 2000 International Airport. Among the world's busiest airports, McCarran was ranked eighth in 1994 traffic volume by the international Airports Council in

Washington, D.C. If you and your family travel to Las Vegas by air, this is where you'll land.

With more than 88,500 hotel and motel rooms to choose from, you're not likely to find yourselves without shelter in Las Vegas. But which hotel will you choose? Which airline? Which shows and excursions? And how much will it all cost? Maybe you already know exactly how you'll get there, where you'll stay, what you want to see, and what to pack for the trip. If not, this chapter provides some suggestions.

FIRST, SEE A TRAVEL AGENT

Nobody else can save you as much time, money, and frustration as a good travel agent. Nobody else can give you so much specific information at the touch of a few computer keys. Travel agents know exactly where to find the best prices for air travel and hotel accommodations. They know which resorts are offering generous package rates and discounts at the moment and how soon the offers will expire. Rates may change overnight, but your travel agent usually receives up-to-the-minute reports.

In some seasons, you can find surprisingly inexpensive hotel rooms at major resorts—*if* you book your accommodations through an airline that has a package arrangement with that resort at the time you want to be there. Travel agents know which airlines to call. For example, a Chicago couple discovered through a travel agent that three days at a large Las Vegas resort, including airfare from Chicago and a book of coupons, would cost less as a package than their airfare alone booked separately. It's a matter of luck, depending upon the time of year—and a travel agent can enhance your luck.

One travel agency in Dallas, Texas, says Las Vegas is a favorite year-round destination for nearly 30 percent of its customers. Most of these are single travelers and couples, who find bargain rates on group charter flights offering package vacations. Now some Texans are discovering the city's attractions as a family destination. Travel agents are ready to help them find the best airfares and room rates.

OR, MANAGE IT ON YOUR OWN

If you'd rather be your own travel agent, now is the time to start some detailed research. You've made a head start by reading this book, but you can make your trip even easier by collecting maps and brochures right away.

Much more than a brochure, the *Las Vegas Official Visitors Guide* published by the Las Vegas Convention & Visitors Authority is a glossy magazine packed with useful information about the city and some of its Nevada neighbors: Laughlin, Stateline, Jean, Mesquite, Henderson, Boulder City, and North Las Vegas. Updated twice a year, the guide provides lists of hotels, motels, restaurants, showrooms, and events scheduled at the time of your visit. It describes all the main attractions on and off the Strip, including side trips to places like the Valley of Fire and Lake Mead. A special *Ethnic Guide* celebrates the city's cultural diversity.

In more than a hundred pages, the *Official Visitors Guide* gives you a concise overall view of the city's vacation possibilities. Simplified maps help you find your way around. Advertisers in the guide will send you more free information if you fill out and mail an inquiry card tucked into the magazine. To receive a copy of the *Las Vegas Official Visitors Guide,* you can write, call, or fax:

Las Vegas Convention & Visitors Authority
3150 Paradise Road
Las Vegas, NV 89109-9096
(702) 892-7575; fax: (702) 892-7555

If you're a member of the **American Automobile Association** (AAA) you already know about their helpful tour books and maps for almost anywhere you want to go. Your local AAA office can help you plan a trip to Las Vegas, even if you're not driving. They'll even make airline and hotel reservations. For airline or Amtrak tickets, hotel rooms, and car rentals, phone the **AAA Travel Agency** at (800) 352-1955. If you want just hotel rooms, call the **AAA Reservation Service** at (800) 272-2155. The AAA map of Las Vegas is free to members and it's great insurance against getting lost in a rented car.

The AAA *California / Nevada Tour Book* contains a detailed eight-page introduction to Las Vegas attractions with a brief history, simplified map, and ten more pages of hotel and motel accommodations in the city. This comprehensive lodging list includes AAA rating symbols, from one to four diamonds, and current room rates. Most prices quoted are "subject to change," but some are "guaranteed" or "AAA Special Value Rates."

A separate booklet, published by the Automobile Club of Southern California, deals exclusively with **Las Vegas and Laughlin**. Compact enough to carry in a purse or pocket, the 128-page book lists sports and recreation areas, campgrounds, annual events, and activities for children as well as the usual lodging and restaurant directories. Handy maps, a list of phone numbers, and an index to points of interest make this a useful take-along reference.

Your local AAA office may have copies of this guide, *Las Vegas and Laughlin, Nevada*. If not, you can call or write to:

Auto Club of Southern California
P.O. Box 2890
Los Angeles, CA 90051
(213) 741-3571

Another valuable source of background information is
Nevada, the state's official magazine. Edited and writ-
ten for residents and tourists, the magazine publishes
lively articles about Nevada people, places, and history.
Photo essays offer close-up glimpses of places you'll want
to include in your itinerary. The **Nevada Events** section
in each issue offers entertainer profiles, restaurant directories, and detailed schedules of happenings around
the state. Vacation tips are a specialty. Pick up a copy on
a newsstand in Nevada, or get in touch with the magazine's Las Vegas office: (702) 486-7334; fax (702) 486-
7904. For a subscription, contact the main office:

Nevada **Magazine**
1800 Highway 50 East, Suite 200
Carson City, NV 89710-0005
(800) 669-1002
(702) 687-5416; fax (702) 687-6159

One little brochure is so useful that Nevada author
David Toll called it "the most important piece of paper
for a parent to have in Las Vegas." Writing in *Nevada*
magazine about his own experiences in Las Vegas with
four children and their mother, Toll recommended this
folder as "your best guide to non-casino kid activities in
and out of town."

He's right. The **M.A.I.N. Association** (Museums and
Attractions in Nevada) distributes the most compact and
comprehensive free list of places to see and things to do
in and around Las Vegas. On both sides of a single long

sheet of paper, folded into five sections, the editors have managed to pack a mini-directory of helpful addresses and telephone numbers. They even saved room for a numbered location map. You'll find copies of the *M.A.I.N. Attractions* brochure at tourist counters all over town. Ahead of time, you can ask the Las Vegas Convention & Visitors Authority (page 218) to send you a copy along with your *Official Visitors Guide*. Since the M.A.I.N. Association is a nonprofit alliance of museums and attractions, there's no central telephone number. You can write to:

Museums and Attractions in Nevada
3305 W. Spring Mountain Road #60
Las Vegas, NV 89102

If you're timing your trip to coincide with a special event in Las Vegas, or if you just want to know what games, competitions, and special exhibitions are scheduled at the time you'll be there, a central source of information is:

Las Vegas Events
2030 E. Flamingo Road #200
Las Vegas, NV 89119
(702) 731-2115; fax (702) 731-9965

Now, armed with a stack of maps and guidebooks, you're ready to make room reservations. If you feel overwhelmed by the number of decisions to be made and the number of choices available, it's not too late to ask for expert help.

TIME SAVERS

In the Yellow Pages of your local telephone book, you may find a list of hotel reservation services with toll-free

numbers to call. Major hotel chains with Las Vegas prop-
erties can tell you about regular room rates and seasonal
packages. They don't charge anything extra to make
reservations. Other reservation services may charge a
fee, as theater ticket brokers do, but the only way to be
sure about this is to ask when you call. Here are a few
sources:

Hilton Reservations *(worldwide)* (800) 445-8667

Marriott Hotels, Resorts, Suites (800) 228-9290

Sheraton Worldwide Reservations (800) 325-3535

Westin Hotels & Resorts *(worldwide)*
    (800) 228-3000

A-Las Vegas Room-Finders (800) 234-8342

Casino Reservations (800) 959-8842

Citywide Reservations (800) 733-6644

Las Vegas Central Reservations (800) 862-1155

Las Vegas Reservation Center (800) 253-2979

Las Vegas Reservation Network (800) 947-6667

Las Vegas/Laughlin Room Reservations
    (800) 321-5877

Some Las Vegas reservation services advertise in
travel magazines. Be sure to read the fine print. If room
rates seem exceptionally low, they may be "per person"
rates. If the ad specifies a "per room" rate, it could be a
real bargain. A few of these services (Citywide, for example) are wholesale travel companies. They'll tell you
about current package offers and discounts and will sell
you a package including airport pickup, rooms, meals,
shows, rental cars, and other extras. They usually offer a
choice of room-only or package plans. Travel agents

often use these services and can tell you which are most reliable.

Las Vegas has some of the largest resort hotels in the world and more hotel and motel rooms than any other city in the United States. In the earlier chapters of this book, you've read about the biggest and newest resorts. Other comfortable hotels (some of them luxurious) and dozens of motels are listed in the AAA tour book and other directories. Among all those rooms, you'll find the ones that suit you, your family, and your budget.

HOW MUCH WILL IT COST?

This is always a tricky question. So much depends upon where you're starting from, how long you'll stay, what kind of accommodations and restaurants you choose, how many people are in your family, their ages, and their tastes.

The Toll family of six—two parents and four children, ages three, seven, eleven, and seventeen—spent $200 a day for two rooms at Excalibur, all meals, and sight-seeing. This budget took careful planning and determination.

"Our biggest expense was food," David Toll reported. "Dining out as a group was hugely time-, money-, and energy-consuming, so we packed groceries in ice chests and picnicked. We made dining out a special treat." Toll's advice to other parents is: "Bring your bucks."

Actual rates for hotel rooms don't always match those listed in tour guides. You can pay less if you shop carefully. A recent survey made for the Las Vegas Convention & Visitors Authority showed that only 43 percent of visitors staying in hotels and motels were paying the listed rate. Others surveyed (27 percent) had bought hotel or airline packages that included rooms, or were paying a tour group rate. Another 5 percent received convention or company rates, 3 percent were given casino discounts, and 4 percent paid nothing at all. (Strange at it may seem, the most luxurious suites in Las Vegas are often complimentary, or "comps," offered to high-rolling gamblers—guests of the casinos expecting to win their money.)

The same survey showed that 57 percent of visitors who *didn't* buy a travel package paid $50 or less per night for their rooms. These statistical visitors (the survey identifies them as "visitors who actually spent money") paid $20.82 per person per day for food and drink and $20.04 per day for taxis and buses. For the whole trip, they spent another $48.10 for sight-seeing, $55.82 for shows, and $128.38 for shopping.

If all these figures are as confusing to you as they are to most of us, just remember the travel agents. They really do make travel simpler.

GETTING THERE IS PART
OF THE ADVENTURE

Whether you make your own reservations or let a travel agent do it, you and your family will decide whether you want to travel by plane, train, bus, or car. The decision will be influenced, of course, by distance, time, and money. Air travel to Las Vegas from New York (2,591 air miles) or Chicago (1,866 air miles) is a lot more economical than driving. Los Angeles, on the other hand, is just 288 miles away. Most visitors from Southern California make the five-and-a-half-hour drive in their own cars.

According to that much-quoted survey, 44 percent of visitors arrive in Las Vegas by plane. Almost as many,

40 percent, travel by car, motorcycle, or truck. Another 11 percent come by bus, and the remaining 5 percent use recreational vehicles. Train travelers weren't counted in this survey, but some vacationers still choose railroads ahead of airlines and highways.

If you love trains, **Amtrak's** *Desert Wind* from Los Angeles will deliver you directly to the Union Plaza hotel in downtown Las Vegas. From other areas, it's best to check current schedules. Recent cutbacks have eliminated railroad service from some places. For specific information, call Amtrack at (800) 872-7245.

Greyhound Bus Lines allows you to enjoy the desert scenery without the strain of desert driving. You can even nap en route. Reservations aren't necessary, and tickets on some western routes include casino coupons. If you live within a day's drive from Las Vegas, and if you can spare the time to make a bus trip part of your vacation, it's worth considering. Find out more by calling Greyhound at (800) 231-2222.

Recreational vehicles are popular with families who like to bring their own hotel rooms on wheels. Las Vegas is ready to accommodate them in spacious RV parks. You can get a complete list of these parks from AAA. Here are three popular RV parks, two of them right on the Strip:

Circusland, with 370 sites next door to Circus Circus Hotel and Casino, has its own swimming pool, playground, grocery store, and Laundromat. For reservations call (702) 794-3757.

Hacienda Camperland has 363 sites adjoining the Hacienda Hotel at the south end of the Strip. Campers find hot showers, tennis courts, and picnic tables as well as a pool and playground. Call (702) 891-8243.

Sam's Town, outside the city on Boulder Highway, is the biggest RV Park in the area. Within a few steps of

Sam's Town casino, shops, restaurants, and bowling center, it has 500 sites and the usual RV amenities. Call (702) 454-8055.

If you're traveling by car, keep in mind the hazards of desert driving in summer. No matter where you're driving from, you'll cross miles of desert before you reach Las Vegas. Be sure to have your car checked carefully before you start out. Make sure the engine and cooling system are in good working order, and have the tires inflated properly.

Again, AAA is your best source of advice for a car trip. They'll give you a page of "Desert Driving Hints," which includes wise words about what to do if your car becomes disabled. ("We advise extreme caution in accepting help from anyone you do not know.")

HOW FAR IN ADVANCE TO PLAN?

The more you plan ahead, the less you'll have to worry about at the last minute. Three months isn't too far in advance to start making hotel and airline reservations, especially if you're planning a summer trip. When schools close for the summer, Las Vegas hotels, motels, and theme resorts are packed with family vacationers.

Most Las Vegas visitors—according to that now-familiar survey—do plan ahead. Their foresightedness varies widely, from same-day to ninety days in advance. Among those surveyed, nearly half (49 percent) made hotel reservations more than a month ahead, and 19 percent started three months in advance. Almost 90 percent of the sample said they'd planned their trip at least a week ahead of time.

There was a time when Las Vegas hotels expected to greet spur-of-the-moment visitors every day. In a recent series of media ads asking, "Hey, why not?" the Convention & Visitors Authority recognized the persistent appeal of impulsive travel to Las Vegas. Unscheduled visitors are still welcome, but they don't always find first-choice rooms and they're likely to pay more than careful planners do. Besides, it's a secure feeling to have rooms waiting when you arrive at the end of a long trip.

WHAT WILL WE WEAR IN LAS VEGAS?

You don't need a fashion consultant to tell you what to wear in this informal holiday city. In amusement parks, hotel lobbies, restaurants, tour buses, and on the street, you'll see everything from shorts and jeans to business suits and Indian saris. The dominant theme is casual, relaxed, comfortable.

Plan for the season and consider what you'll be doing each day. Will you spend most of your time on the Strip, in and out of air-conditioned buildings and shopping malls? Splashing in swimming pools? Will you be hiking in the desert? Sailing on the lake? Maybe a little of each?

April through October will be warm, sometimes hot, but you're likely to find a nip in the air from November through March, especially at night. A light sweater will be welcome, at times, in any season. (The arctic chill in some air-conditioned restaurants seems coldest when the outdoor summer temperature is above 110°F.) Whatever the time of year, the only universal advice is: bring comfortable walking shoes.

If your children are old enough to select the clothes they wear to school every day, they can do at least some of their own packing. You can keep a careful parental eye on the process, but you'll be spared a lot of future headaches if they know they're responsible for their own clothes. Stress the wisdom of packing *less*. Nobody needs a different costume for every day and night. You'll find yourself wearing your favorite jeans, slacks, skirts, and T-shirts over and over again. Each member of the family may want to take one "dress-up" outfit to wear to a show or dinner in a special restaurant, but you'll see others there in their casual everyday sight-seeing clothes.

A few easy-care pieces can be kept fresh with a little bedtime washing in the hotel basin. If you object to a bathroom full of dripping socks and underwear, ask if there's a laundry room for guests in the hotel. Neighborhood Laundromats are listed in the Yellow Pages.

Once all the suitcases are packed, is everybody ready to go? Enjoy!

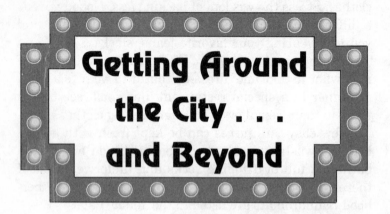

Getting Around
the City . . .
and Beyond

Las Vegas traffic—especially on the Strip—is as unpredictable and frustrating as traffic in any other busy resort city. At times it flows smoothly, then for a while seems hopelessly stalled. Some delays can be blamed on detours around construction sites, where new roads are being created to drain off congestion. Once this work is completed, Las Vegas may look even more like a science fiction City of the Future.

A brand-new six-lane tunnel under Las Vegas Boulevard and an elevated overpass above Interstate 15 are part of the $93 million Desert Inn Road Super Arterial, scheduled to open sometime in 1996. Meanwhile, be prepared to wait at busy intersections during rush hours and on weekends. Arriving or leaving town by car on a holiday weekend can be nightmarish. Whether or not you do the driving, patience always helps.

Even more help is expected soon from the city's upgraded traffic control system. By the end of 1995, a series of video cameras will be in place at key intersections around the city to relay signals to the Downtown Traffic Control Center. When traffic snarls develop, computers can change signals on short notice to break the gridlock.

Local taxi drivers know these streets and traffic patterns. City buses cover major routes. Even if you travel in your own car or rent one at the airport, it can't hurt to know about the city's public transportation options. Suppose you've just arrived by plane. . . .

HOW DO WE GET TO OUR HOTEL?

When you land at McCarran International Airport, you're so close to the south end of the Strip that you can see the distinctive outlines of Excalibur, the MGM Grand, and the Luxor pyramid on the near horizon. You're just three and a half miles from the Las Vegas Convention Center (mid-Strip) and five miles from downtown, the original Glitter Gulch.

Some resorts send their own vans to pick up hotel guests at the airport. If you're not sure about your hotel, ask at the transportation desk near the baggage claim area or call the hotel. You may find it listed on an illustrated board with free direct-line phones.

Taxicabs will take you anywhere you want to go, twenty-four hours a day. If your hotel is on the Strip, the ride from the airport will cost $7 to $10. For Fremont Street and downtown hotels, you'll pay $15 to $18. As soon as the meter is switched on, it registers $2.20 (the official base rate) and ticks away, adding 30 cents for each fifth of a mile and another 30 cents for each minute of waiting time. Rates are the same for any licensed cab in the area. If you don't see a meter, pick another cab. Unlicensed taxis often overcharge.

Predictable fares are an advantage on **Bell Trans Airport Shuttle Service**: $3.50 per person to the Strip and $4.75 to downtown hotels. Children pay full fare on the shuttle, so you may find a taxi cheaper for the whole family, depending upon the size of your family and how far you're going. (Taxis charge the same amount for a trip whether they carry one person or five.) Shuttle vans make scheduled runs, picking up and dropping off passengers at most hotels. At the airport, you'll find a shuttle bus near the baggage claim area, outside Door 9. For a return trip from your hotel, phone Bell Trans to reserve space: (702) 739-7990.

Citizens Area Transit (CAT) operates a special Strip Shuttle from the airport to the Convention Center, with stops along the way. The fare is $1.50 for adults and 50 cents for riders five to seventeen years old. Children under five ride free when accompanied by an adult. CAT is very convenient if you're not carrying a lot of luggage.

If you've just won the sweepstakes and want to make a grandiose gesture, **Presidential Limousine Service** will take you to your hotel in Las Vegas style—for a price. A stretch limousine big enough for six passengers costs $42 per hour; a superstretch with room for eight costs $65 per hour, and there's a one-hour minimum charge for each. An ad for the company promises a long list of extras:

- a complimentary bottle of champagne
- a long stem rose for the lady
- a cellular phone for the use of our clients
- a complimentary stocked bar of cocktail mixers
- a chauffeur attired in a formal tuxedo and cap
- the convenience of accepting all three major credit cards

All this, in addition to "standard amenities" like color TV, stereo radio, and VCR. To reserve your Presidential chariot, call (702) 731-5577.

Bell Trans, the same company that operates the airport shuttle, also offers chauffered stretch limousines at $33 per hour and Lincoln Town Cars at $25, each with a one-hour minimum. If you're traveling with a large group, they'll rent you a twenty-passenger bus with driver for $36 per hour. Call for reservations: (702) 739-7990 or (702) 385-5466.

In the real world, most visitors to Las Vegas get around by less flamboyant means. Maybe you reserved a rental car for your vacation. If it's part of a package plan, you've been told where to pick it up. Major car rental companies have desks near the baggage claim at the airport. They'll give you a map of Las Vegas and will direct you to their own shuttle buses for direct transportation to your car. From there, you're on your own.

To make car reservations ahead of time, call one of the toll-free numbers listed under Automobile Rentals in the Yellow Pages of your phone book. You'll find dozens of car-rental companies listed, but here are a few of those mentioned in the *Las Vegas Official Visitors Guide:*

Airport Discount Rent-A-Car (800) 221-4447

Alamo Rent-A-Car (800) 327-9633

Avis Rent-A-Car (800) 831-2847

Budget Rent-A-Car (800) 527-0700

Dollar Rent-A-Car (800) 800-4000

Enterprise Rent-A-Car (800) 325-8007

Hertz Rent-A-Car (800) 654-3131

National Car Rental (Interrent) (800) 227-7368

Thrifty Rent-A-Car (800) 367-2277

U.S. Rent-A-Car (800) 777-9377

PARK THE CAR AND START EXPLORING

Five minutes after you and your family climb into your rented car, you'll be driving along the Las Vegas Strip. If you're staying at one of the big resorts between the airport and Spring Mountain Road, you'll be there before you know it. Free parking is easy to find. Just look for signs near the hotel entrance, directing you to valet parking or self-parking. Both are free, but some visitors prefer to park their own cars so they'll know where to find them when they're ready to go out.

Valet parking saves you a lot of trouble when you're new in town, checking in for the first time with children and luggage. As soon as you drive up to the entrance, a bellman will help you unload the car and will direct you to the registration desk while a parking attendant disappears with your car. Most people tip the parking attendant a dollar or two when the car is returned. Others offer a tip in advance, too, since the car may be returned by a different person. (If the attendant waits around after the car is unloaded, you can take the hint. If he or she rushes away before you can bring out your wallet, you know it's okay to wait.) The bellman will appreciate a few dollars for delivering your suitcases to your room. A dollar a bag is standard.

Tipping is voluntary, of course, but it's part of "getting around" in Las Vegas. You can be prepared by keeping a supply of one-dollar bills in your wallet. A few guidelines compiled for the Convention & Visitors Authority suggest some customary figures:

- **Hotel maids** expect $1 a day at the end of your visit.
- Add 15 to 20 percent for the **waiter** or **waitress** when you pay a restaurant bill.

- **Swimming pool attendants** get 50 cents to a dollar if they bring you towels and lounge chairs.
- **Taxi drivers** expect $1 to $2 for a direct route; more if the driver helps with luggage.
- **Tour guides** receive $1 to $2 per person in your party at the end of the trip.

Showroom tips can be tricky. Some of the new family-oriented showrooms include a tip in the price of the ticket, so you don't even have to think about it. Because your seat number is printed on the ticket, there's no need to bribe anybody to find you a better one. In the old days, headwaiters in restaurant-style showrooms expected $5 to $20 for escorting a party to a front table—or any table at all. In some resorts, you still find dinner shows with unassigned seating. Let your conscience be your guide.

GETTING AROUND ON THE STRIP

There's so much for kids to do at resorts like the MGM Grand, Excalibur, Luxor, the Mirage, Treasure Island, and Circus Circus that some families have to remind themselves to go out and see the rest of the Strip. The best way to see it is on foot, but don't be surprised if you discover distances much greater than you expected. A stroll from Luxor to Grand Slam Canyon looks like nothing at all on the map. The reality is a three-mile hike on crowded sidewalks. This is not so awfully far if you're just walking, but it takes forever if you stop anywhere for sight-seeing; and for little legs, of course, it is much farther.

There's no denying the convenience of having a car for getting around in Las Vegas, but who wants to spend vacation days getting in and out of casino garages on the Strip? It's possible to save time with public transportation and still do plenty of sight-seeing between stops.

The newest time-saver, unveiled in the summer of 1995, is an elevated **monorail service** between the MGM Grand and Bally's Hotel, a mile away. Two air-conditioned six-car trains cover the distance in about three minutes, carrying some four thousand passengers in an hour. Now there's talk of a future monorail linking the MGM with McCarran International Airport. Other hotels may eventually become part of the monorail system.

Since Treasure Island is part of the Mirage property, it's easy to walk from one resort to the other, but it's fun to ride their brass-trimmed **shuttle-trolley**. The air-conditioned ride is free and quick, giving you a brief view of the palm trees and neon on the Strip.

At ground level, the city-operated **Strip Trolley** travels up and down Las Vegas Boulevard, stopping at the main entrances of all major hotels. It also stops at Wet 'n' Wild and the Fashion Show Mall. Trolleys run every day, 9:30 A.M. to 2 A.M. You can catch one approximately every thirty minutes. Sometimes you'll wait longer if a trolley is delayed in heavy traffic, and cars can be very crowded during rush hours and holidays. Fares change, but the recent rate has been $1.10, whether you're going one block or traveling the whole length of the Strip. For current fares and schedules, call (702) 382-1404.

Citizens Area Transit (CAT) is the Las Vegas valley's public transportation system. Hundreds of local residents use these buses to get to work, schools, church, and shopping. So can you. The Strip route operates twenty-four hours a day, and most other CAT buses operate from 5:30 A.M. to 1:30 A.M. every day, including holidays. Some buses go to the factory outlet stores south of the Strip and to Henderson and Boulder City. For specific fares, call (702) 228-7433, or pick up a route map and schedule at the **Downtown Transportation Center**, 300 North Casino Center Boulevard. (Maps and schedules are available in Spanish too.)

GUIDED SIGHT-SEEING TOURS

Escorted introductions to Las Vegas are a great way to skim the main attractions within a predictable time. On a city tour, you can make the rounds with a group, find out where things are, and decide which places you and your family want to revisit at leisure. Outside the city, put away your road maps and let the driver do all the work.

Several tour companies offer to show you Las Vegas highlights in a morning, afternoon, or all-day sight-seeing expedition by bus. Some will take you up for an eagle's perspective from a helicopter, small plane, or hot-air balloon. They'll pick you up at your hotel and bring you back within a specified time. These tours are advertised in entertainment magazines. You can ask the concierge, look for brochures at the hotel desk, or call one of the following tour operators.

Gray Line Tours schedules a variety of daily excursions in and around the city. They'll give you an efficient get-acquainted Mini-City tour (Number 10) lasting approximately six hours, noon to 6 P.M., which includes the Strip, Nevada State Museum in Lorenzi Park, Glitter Gulch, the Ethel M Chocolate Factory in Henderson, homes of the stars, and highlights in between. Other Gray Line tours range from a Hoover Dam Express to an overnight trip to the Grand Canyon. Call for details and prices, (702) 384-1234.

Ray & Ross Sightseeing Tours creates new itineraries to suit changing demands. Look for discount coupons in their magazine ads. For latest schedules and prices, call (702) 646-4661.

Las Vegas Adventure Tours will take you skydiving, bungee-jumping, or off the beaten path by jeep, plane, and watercraft to places you might miss on your own. Find out what's possible: (702) 564-5452.

Kids VIP Tours will escort small groups of children, six years or older, to theme parks and Strip attractions while their parents take a break. Licensed guides have beepers, and groups are limited to six children. Expeditions travel on foot or by city buses, and souvenir shopping is part of the itinerary. Lunch and ride tickets are included in the cost: day tours, $65; night tours, $80. Call for details: (702) 243-0309.

The **American Balloon Company** shows you the city, desert, and mountains from the basket of a ten-story-high hot-air balloon floating above the scene. Certified pilots maneuver the balloon through one-hour flights, morning or evening. Air-shy adventurers can go up as high as 150 feet on a tethered balloon. For reservations call (800) 223-4373.

Adventure Airline arranges private charter flights. Their telephone number is the same as **Canyon Flyers** for air and ground tours of the Grand Canyon: (702) 293-3446.

Air Nevada Airlines will tell you about their scheduled air service and sight-seeing tours to the Grand Canyon, Bryce Canyon, and Monument Valley. They also provide charter service throughout the Southwest. Call (702) 736-8900 or (800) 634-6377.

Scenic Airlines schedules half-day, full-day, and overnight trips to the Grand Canyon, Bryce Canyon, and Monument Valley aboard a nineteen-passenger

Vistaliner aircraft with panoramic windows. Call (702) 739-1900.

Helicop Tours will give you a custom-tailored itinerary. Ask them about a trip to the Grand Canyon with a picnic inside the River Gorge. Call (702) 736-0606.

Lake Mead Air specializes in scenic flights to the Grand Canyon, taking off from Boulder City. Phone for updated fares and times: (702) 293-1848.

Black Canyon River Raft Tours will take you on a four-hour expedition down the Colorado River on a big inflated raft, with a picnic lunch along the way. Expect to get a bit wet, but you won't be battling any white-water rapids. They'll pick you up at your hotel and bring you back. For times and prices, call (702) 293-3776.

WHAT CAN YOU DO FOR AN ENCORE?

When you've seen so much that you think there's nothing left to explore on your next trip to Las Vegas, just take a look at all the construction in progress. The city grows and changes so fast that many travel publications become obsolete before the ink dries. A recent federal census shows Nevada as the nation's fastest-growing state. Las Vegas, according to other figures, is Nevada's fastest-growing city.

In the first section of this book you read about some of the newest and biggest resorts and attractions on the Las Vegas Strip. Within the next two years, visitors will be crowding into newer and bigger ones. Some will open even sooner.

New York, New York is expected to open in 1996 on an eighteen-acre site at the corner of Tropicana Avenue and the Strip. Replicas of the Statue of Liberty, the Empire State Building, and Coney Island (complete with roller coaster) will be part of a Big Apple theme in the entertainment center of a fifteen-hundred-room casino-resort. MGM Grand, Inc., and Primadonna Resorts, Inc., are joint venturers in the project.

Star Trek: The Experience will open at the Las Vegas Hilton late in 1996 to celebrate the thirtieth anniversary of the original *Star Trek* television show. This twenty-two-minute interactive adventure will take you aboard *Starfleet*—or the alien ship, if you choose—into a race through the galaxies. Paramount Parks designed the high-tech adventure and will operate it as a joint venture with Hilton Hotels.

Beau Rivage, Stephen Wynn's lavish new addition to his string of Mirage Resorts, soon will take shape on an island in the middle of a lake being dug on 110 acres once occupied by the Dunes Hotel. The fifty-story hotel will have three thousand rooms and a rumored price tag of $900 million. We'll have to wait until 1997 to see those marble bathrooms.

Victoria, a three-thousand-room hotel-casino with a turn-of-the-century theme, is another Stephen Wynn project for Mirage Resorts in partnership with Gold Strike Resorts. It's coming in 1997, about a mile north of the Mirage on the Strip.

More big plans are in the works for **Circus Circus Enterprises**, recent purchasers of the Hacienda Hotel at the south end of the Strip. Rumors come and go about **Desert World**, a possible new attraction near the **Desert Inn**, now owned by ITT Corp., along with **Caesars World**.

And that's just the beginning. Stay tuned.

CHAPTER 16

Special Arrangements

Nobody *expects* an emergency, but it's comforting to know what to do if somebody gets sick, loses a wallet, or suddenly sees flames on the road ahead. Assume your Las Vegas vacation is going to be absolutely perfect, but in case you run into unexpected problems, we've rounded up a few telephone numbers to help you cope.

We've also discovered some helpful sources of information for people traveling with wheelchairs, families in search of religious services, and those who included the family pet in their vacation plans. Special arrangements are possible for parents looking for a reliable baby-sitter when they'd like to go out for a festive evening on their own. And if you want to rent a motor home for a week or weekend in the desert, or just do laundry at weird hours, a few more phone numbers could be useful.

WHEN YOU NEED A DOCTOR

If it's a real emergency, dial **9-1-1** right away. Or, from your hotel room, dial the hotel operator. Most hotels can send a doctor in a hurry. If you know you have to get the patient to a hospital emergency room, call one of the following.

Desert Springs Hospital
2075 East Flamingo Road
(702) 733-8800

24-hour emergency treatment: **(702) 369-7647**

**Sunrise Children's Hospital and
Sunrise Hospital & Medical Center**
3186 South Maryland Parkway
(702) 731-8000

Emergency Room: **(702) 731-8080**
Poison Control Center: (702) 732-4989

University Medical Center
1800 West Charleston Boulevard
(702) 383-2000

Emergency Room: **(702) 383-2211**
Quick Care Center: (702) 383-2074
Physician referral: (702) 383-2060

Valley Hospital Medical Center
620 Shadow Lane
(702) 388-4000

24-hour emergency treatment: **(702) 388-4500**
Doctor referral: (702) 388-4852

Doctors on Call
In the Imperial Palace Hotel
3535 Las Vegas Boulevard South
8th floor, Suite 1
(702) 735-3600

If the patient feels well enough to go out for immediate treatment, **Doctors on Call** is right on the Strip, open around-the-clock, seven days a week, and you don't have to make an appointment. Just walk in or call for free shuttle service to and from your hotel. The complex has its own x-ray laboratory and some medications available. If it's a real emergency, a doctor will make a house call.

EMERGENCY NUMBERS

Air Ambulance America *(airport)* (800) 262-8526

Ambulance Emergency (702) 384-3400

Crisis Response *(drug related)* (702) 364-1111

Desert Rescue, Inc. (702) 641-3749

Respiratory Support (702) 733-7370

Las Vegas Fire Department (702) 385-3000

Metro Police (702) 795-3111

Poison Information Center (702) 732-4989

To report a forest fire (702) 647-5090

A FEW MORE USEFUL NUMBERS

Airport Information (702) 261-5743

Airport Parking (702) 261-5121

Citizens Area Transit (CAT buses)
(702) 228-7433

Las Vegas Transit System (702) 228-7433

Highway Patrol (702) 385-0311

Road Conditions (702) 486-3116

Tourist Information (702) 892-7575

Weather (702) 736-3854

LAS VEGAS FOR WHEELCHAIR TRAVELERS

In 1973 Douglas Conner's motorcycle collided with a truck and his spine was injured, paralyzing his arms and legs. Since then he has used a wheelchair, but he hasn't let it slow him down in Las Vegas. As a subsitute teacher in Clark County public schools, Conner sees the city from a resident's point of view and finds it remarkably wheelchair-friendly.

Even before he moved to Nevada from Colorado in 1992, Conner had visited Las Vegas often. Each time, he looked for hotels, restaurants, museums, and entertainment attractions accessible to people with physical disabilities. Over the years, he was pleased to find new hotels in Las Vegas being built to comply with standards set by the Americans with Disabilities Act (the 1990 federal law assuring the disabled that they must have access to employment, services, and public buildings, including hotels and restaurants).

Impressed with the growing accessibility he found in Las Vegas, Conner wanted to tell others about it. So he began a systematic survey, visiting sixty-five hotels and motels in and around Las Vegas, rating them all according to a specific list of requirements. He tested taxicabs and buses, joined sight-seeing tours, attended sporting events, and explored state parks, observing everything from what he calls a "wheelchair point-of-view."

The results of his survey became Conner's travel book, *The Challenged Traveler's Guide to Las Vegas,* a ninety-eight-page paperback packed with indispensable information for travelers with disabilities. He tells which hotels have free valet parking, entrance doors that open and close automatically, and rooms equipped with door handles as opposed to hard-to-manage knobs. Recalling his own past experiences with bathroom doors too narrow to allow wheelchair access, he examined hotel bathrooms, looking for rails in bathtubs, raised toilets, and handles—not knobs—on doors and faucets.

Wheelchair access was Conner's initial concern, but he also included hearing-impaired and visually impaired travelers in his search, looking for braille symbols in hotel elevators and Telecommunication Devices for the Deaf (TDD) in guest rooms. He discovered resort restaurants with menus in braille or on cassettes, and hotel rooms with closed-captioned television and Alert Plus security systems for door and fire alarms.

In *The Challenged Traveler's Guide to Las Vegas,* Conner lists hotels according to his rating system, giving four stars to those who comply with all or most of his requirements. He also lists telephone numbers for helpful private transportation, taxi, and rental companies that supply wheel-accessible vans. More useful phone numbers are listed for service and support groups such as the Nevada Association for the Handicapped.

You'll find Conner's guidebook in libraries and bookstores. If your bookstore doesn't have it, they can order it for you through Baker and Taylor, a national book distributor, for $10.

To keep up with the many changes affecting disabled travelers in Las Vegas and southern Nevada, Conner also publishes a quarterly information update, the

Challenged Traveler's Newsletter. To get a copy, send a stamped, self-addressed envelope to:

CT Newsletter
2756 North Green Valley Parkway, Suite 476
Henderson, NV 89014

TRAVELING WITH THE FAMILY PET

Another unusual directory for travelers comes from Arizona author Eileen Barish, who adopted two golden retriever puppies just before she and her husband, Harvey, took off on a two-week vacation through California to Lake Tahoe. She couldn't bear to leave the puppies in a kennel, so she took them along. Traveling with pets, she and Harvey discovered, was easier than they expected.

The puppies, Rosie and Maxwell, turned out to be born travelers, adaptable and enthusiastic. Several years and dozens of trips later, Barish compiled a directory of ten thousand hotels, motels, inns, ranches, and bed-and-breakfasts in the United States where guests with pets are welcome. *Vacationing with Your Pet* lists these "pet-friendly lodgings" state by state, city by city, from Alabama to Wyoming.

In Las Vegas, most of the big resorts do not allow pets, but Barish discovered nineteen hotels and motels that do, including one major family destination—Excalibur. Her list also includes several Best Westerns, a Rodeway Inn near MGM, and Bonnie Springs Old Nevada Motel outside the city. She also lists the Barker Motel (no pun intended?) in North Las Vegas. Entries include addresses, phone numbers, and rates.

Barish's advice isn't limited to dog owners. *Vacationing with Your Pet* includes tips for traveling with cats, too. She anticipates and answers questions about kennels, air travel, health certificates, and what to pack for the pet's trip. If you can't find the book in your hometown bookstore, call (800) 496-2665. It's available for $14.95 from:

Pet-Friendly Publications
P.O. Box 8459
Scottsdale, Arizona 85252

BABY-SITTING SERVICES

What if you and your spouse want to go out for an evening for two? Will the children be safe and happy with anyone else? Many resorts offer child-care services, and some have special programs for school-age children and youths. Ask your hotel desk for recommendations.

At the MGM Grand, for example, the Youth Center is open from 8 A.M. to midnight (see chapter 3, pages 38–40). Trained counselors supervise games and activities in the center and conduct tours of the Grand Adventure theme park for kids six to sixteen. Parents of younger children can ask for a list of reputable baby-sitting services. Youth Center recommendations include:

Around the Clock Child Care (702) 365-1040

Precious Commodities (702) 871-1191

Vegas Valley Babysitting (702) 871-5161

Any of these services will send a licensed sitter to your hotel room. Rates are about the same for all three. Recent prices ranged from $34 for four hours with one or two children to $39 for the same length of time with four children. A four-hour minimum seems to be standard.

TIME OUT FOR FAMILY WORSHIP

Travelers don't leave their faith at home, and many visitors to Las Vegas are surprised to find so many churches in a city with such a notoriously secular reputation. In *Vegas Live and In Person,* a 1989 illustrated tribute to the city, author/photographer Jefferson Graham makes a sweeping statement: "There are more churches per capita in Vegas than in any other city."

It's easy to believe Graham's claim if you look in the Yellow Pages of the Las Vegas telephone book. Nine pages of addresses and phone numbers identify all kinds of churches, from African Methodist and Baha'i Faith to Greek Orthodox and Sikh. The largest number are Mormon (Church of Jesus Christ of Latter Day Saints), a reminder that Nevada was once Brigham Young country, part of Utah in the 1800s. Synagogues and Jewish Temples, listed separately, fill another two columns.

Weekend editions of local newspapers list specific schedules of services at some churches. Most hotels post or provide a list of religious services in the neighborhood, and Las Vegans are happy to welcome strangers to their houses of worship. On the Strip, the popular Guardian Angel Church has become a tourist attraction, drawing crowds every weekend.

LAUNDRY—A VERY PRACTICAL MATTER

Even on vacation, somebody in the family has to think about keeping clothes clean. When your children are about to run out of clean socks, underwear, jeans, and T-shirts, it's time to confront that overflowing laundry bag and look for help. Some laundries will pick up your bundle and drop off a finished package the next day.

If you'd rather do it yourself and save money, self-service Laundromats are easy to reach from the Strip. The university neighborhood has a lot of them and some are open twenty-four hours. Here are a few to consider.

A Laundromat
1801 East Tropicana Avenue
(702) 736-0503

Cora's Coin Laundry
1097 East Tropicana Avenue
(in University Plaza)
(702) 736-6181

Duds & Suds
820 East Twain Avenue
(Twain-Swenson Plaza)
(702) 732-7737

Advertises video poker, TV,
and "good clean fun."

Launderland
2625 East Tropicana Avenue
Open 24 hours
(702) 454-6177

24 Hours Laundromat
3547 South Maryland Parkway
(across from J.C. Penney)
(702) 893-2424

Two Girls
531 East Sahara Avenue
Open 7 A.M. to 10 P.M.
(702) 369-0817

The Washboard
4137 South Maryland Parkway
Open Monday–Saturday, 7 A.M. to 8 P.M.;
Sunday, 8 A.M. to 6 P.M.
(702) 732-0998

MOTOR HOME RENTALS

Once you've tasted the desert outside Las Vegas, you may love it or hate it but you won't forget it. Writing in *Nevada* magazine, Nevada poet Shaun Griffin explains his own fascination with the bare landscape, welcoming the knowledge that ". . . just beyond the neon borders lies the open space, riding an infinite line in all directions."

If you and your family fall in love with the desert, you'll want to come back again. Some westerners come in their motor homes to camp in the desert. Visitors from the east, arriving by air, often rent motor homes for a weekend, a week, or longer. Before your next trip to Las Vegas, you can find out more about motor home rentals by calling one of these numbers:

B&H RV Center (702) 384-4445 or (800) 890-8194

Bates Motor Home Rental Network
(702) 736-2070 or (800) 446-2283

Cruise America Motor Homes (702) 456-6666

Flamingo RV Valet Center (702) 364-9800

Sahara RV Center (702) 384-8818

Most desert-campers will tell you they always take along a favorite book or two for leisurely reading in solitary moments. What could be more appropriate than an anthology of Nevada poets? In *Desert Wood,* from the University of Nevada Press, forty-nine poets reveal the many facets of their imagination. Much of their work reflects the influence of the desert.

Shaun Griffin, who edited the collection, includes one of his own poems, "A Place of Stone," in which he repeats his reasons for seeking the wilderness: ". . . I come as so many others must, for that which is missing from the stencil of the city." In the same anthology, Kirk Robertson's poem "Driving to Vegas" speaks for every traveler who has ever approached the glittering city for the first time:

> *you wonder*
> *what you'll do*
> *when you reach*
> *the edge*
> *of the map*
>
> *out there*
> *on the horizon*
>
> *all that neon*
>
> *beckoning you*
>
> *in from the dark*

Index